ASCENT

ASCENT

A Practising Manager's GROWTH MANTRA

AMIT CHATTERJEE

PORTFOLIO
PENGUIN

An imprint of Penguin Random House

PORTFOLIO

USA | Canada | UK | Ireland | Australia
New Zealand | India | South Africa | China | Singapore

Portfolio is part of the Penguin Random House group of companies whose addresses can be found at global.penguinrandomhouse.com

Published by Penguin Random House India Pvt. Ltd
4th Floor, Capital Tower 1, MG Road,
Gurugram 122 002, Haryana, India

Penguin
Random House
India

First published by Random House India 2014

10 9 8 7 6 5 4 3 2

ISBN 9788184006230

Typeset in Adobe Garamond by Saanvi Graphics, Noida

Printed at Repro India Limited

www.penguin.co.in

FSC
www.fsc.org
MIX
Paper from responsible sources
FSC® C047271

This is a legitimate digitally printed version of the book and therefore might not have certain extra finishing on the cover.

To my dear parents

Contents

PART 4
The Leader's Arena

PART 5
The Synthesis

PART 6
In Reflection

Foreword

'How should we develop our leaders for the 21st century?' This is a question I am asked almost every week. It is a curiously misguided question—there is only one leader you develop—yourself. Companies and governments don't develop leaders; nor do schools and colleges. Leaders are made when people discover and express their own authority. This is the powerful message of this book, spoken with honest insight by a man who has been there and done it himself. I know—Amit Chatterjee has been a student, colleague, and correspondent of mine for many years and now, with this book, he becomes my teacher too.

Organizations can't develop leaders, but they can make the conditions in which leaders emerge—not always immediately, but a slow-growing impetus can be set in motion; or a pent up readiness can be released by just the right developmental opportunity. There are four ingredients, each of which needs skillful attention: person, perspective, practice and purpose. I'll elaborate a bit on each.

Person: The most potent force is always the person who knows what they want to do and decides to do it. We all grow up more or less adjusted to our social settings, and a good coach or a good friend is one who helps us to recognize the compromises we may no longer want to accept. There is no formula for this, except that it is personal, sometimes unsettling, and necessary.

Perspective: There are few lessons so precious as discovering something new and fresh in your familiar day-to-day world. It transforms mundane activities into a treasuretrove of potential revelations, exciting curiosity and creativity. There are plenty of ways to gain new perspectives—a theory is helpful if it reconfigures the way you see things, but study is not the only way to go at this. Immersing yourself in someone else's world, or inviting another into yours, can be just as challenging. But one thing is for sure: business as usual is very unlikely to give anyone a fresh perspective, so change what you do, how you do it, who you do it with, where you do it.

Practice: I once asked a fitness instructor how best to prepare for a challenging hike carrying a heavy pack up and down mountain tracks. His reply? 'Carry a heavy pack up and down mountain tracks.' People need practice in taking responsibility, nurturing an initiative, and dwelling in the loneliness of command. It's not always best done alone. Two or three people can share the load—in fact most leaders rely on some close associates to help them out, usually the same trusted colleagues over and over. So what should they practise? Well, leadership practices, of course: chairing meetings, representing the organization, negotiating deals, affirming a shared mission, and a myriad other practices that make up the skill-set of a leader. An organization that wants to develop leaders should give plenty of practice in leadership practices.

Purpose: Reminding people of purposes larger than themselves is almost always received as leadership. Leadership is (metaphorically) to stretch outwards and upwards in a way that strengthens the inner and rooted sense of self in the world. The greater fits well into the lesser, because a transcendent purpose can easily find expression in a small and particular act; yet a great enterprise can be ruined by mean and selfish motives. So,the most important aspects of leadership development are to cultivate an expansive spirit, a love of service, and a practical idealism.

Mixing these ingredients isn't so hard, but it's seldom done right. All too often, companies send their high potential staff off to business schools or training adventures where they might get new perspectives and some personal coaching—but when they come back to work there is no plan to help them practice; and less sense of higher purpose. I prefer to see the focus the other way around—encourage people to practise leadership, and then find ways to give them new perspectives and personal attention. That is why I recommend this book: it is unequivocally about purposeful practices of leadership.

Prof. Jonathan Gosling
Professor of Leadership, University
of Exeter and Co-founder of IMPM
June 2014

Do the following statements sound familiar?

- *I need to become an engineer. You don't understand, although I like Psychology, I just can't follow that career stream.*
- *I want to work for an MNC (multinational company). My friends there have a rocking lifestyle.*
- *I need to finish this task by the weekend. My boss expects the report by Monday morning.*
- *No, Anthony does not fit. The boss does not like him. Let us propose Ajay for the Team Lead position.*
- *We need to get an order intake of 5 million by Sept., if you all want to earn your incentives. Anyone doing less than 90% can look for another job.*
- *Just finish the design as per the SOP. You do not need to show off your creativity. We need to meet deadlines and budgets.*
- *We need to raise the productivity. Sub-contract; reduce workforce. No, you cannot invest in automation; we are in a low profit commodity market.*
- *No, we are not measured by market shares. The main KPI is topline growth.*
- *See what adjustments we can make. Talk to the auditors. We can't present the financials as it stands. I can't face the*

investors with this. Arrange a dinner for me with the partner on Thursday, if you can't manage the chief auditor.

- *We have to achieve a 25% growth in EBIT this quarter and repeat that every quarter…God knows for how many years this has to go on. Well, at least the EMI on the new apartment gets paid.*
- *We have to cut our costs by 20% this year. It is a decision from the HO, across all subsidiaries.*
- *I need to join the Riverside Club. I know it is expensive.*
- *We need to change the school. It is too old fashioned. The school where the Gupta kids are going has a swimming pool, a gym, piano classes, what not. They teach three foreign languages.*
- *Sorry, darlings (on phone to kids). Saturday, I have to join the dinner at our club. Okay, we can order the Pizzas you love tonight. Fine, I will get the drumsticks from KFC on my way back. Bye.*
- *I need to go to the Bombay Store. Anjali got some fabulous vases from there. Yes baby, we will get some new Games for you too. The Kids section is on the floor below only.*
- *Sorry, I could not finish it. The weekend was too tight. Piano lessons for our daughter, then a dash for her tuitions; you know she has her board exams next year. Evening, we had to invite our friends over as it was our turn for the fortnightly party. Sunday was hectic. Shopping, swimming lessons for my son and wife. Of course, I help her with the dinner. I will finish it on the plane tonight.*
- *Interesting topic; it would be nice if you can send the article over email to me. No, not on my Gmail; I hardly get time to check my personal mails. You know this email disease*

in companies. I have 886 unread mails in my inbox. The smartphones have made it easier to read and respond on the go. Sorry, got to take this call. 'Hello, yeah, am on the way…'

- *I tell you, this 'Doctor At Your Door' service in India is a boon for us NRIs; now, my Mom and Dad have no problems. They have to just call this number and a doctor is at their doorstep in 30 mins. I used to be so worried about my parents.*
- *Politicians are only worried about the next election. Everybody is looking at money overnight. Forget it! You cannot get Statesmen like Mahatma Gandhi, Shastriji, Sardar Patel, or Netaji Subhash anymore who think about the next generation.*

All the above are daily 'reactions' we hear from people we meet, know, and even love—including ourselves. The basic stimuli for all these reactions comes from either striving for some short-term need fulfilment or living up to someone else's expectations.

I believe we would not react as above if we were to think of where we want to reach in the long run. If we were to pause a bit and conjure a vision, use our knowledge and experience. We would instead Decide to lead our life in the way we have Chosen to. We would not then fall prey to short-term motivators or expectations!

in companies. I have [illegible] my [illegible]. They [illegible] contemporaries have made it as far as CEO and [illegible] [illegible] to talk [illegible]

Preface

I am no Larry Bossidy, Narayana Murthy, Peter Senge, or Ram Charan. I am a brown, sallow cheeked 'Made in India' Indian, still working for a company where I have been for two decades. In my 32 years in the industry, I worked the last 29 in just 2 companies. Yes, I did play many different roles in these three decades and I am thankful for what I learnt till now as a human being as well as a practising manager. I do not have an MBA and never worked for haloed companies like GE, Unilever, or even Wipro. Few years back, I thought I had a story to tell, some experiences to share that could help other managers like me in their lives. This book is a tryst with that objective.

I am like thousands of others who had no option but to become a manager and survive. I never thought of becoming a professional manager, but realized some years back that I have. Today, I run a successful Indian subsidiary of a German technology company. I get 7 emails a day, less than 4 calls on my handy and make about 2. My managers and I have fun and the 20 man company I joined as a Sales Manager 20 years back is a market leader in most businesses with hardly any attrition at all levels of managerial positions. Most of the managers are home grown and few are already participating in global management functions.

Like most of my readers, I too learnt about management or leadership on the job; observing others, reading books by, and from, a few management development programs. Like them, I too raised my family, did my duties, and can still see the glint in my eyes during the morning shave. I am more like the guy who always scans the airport book stalls to find a book that could help him do his job better or offer hints to lead his life towards a happier end. I worked with different industries like building materials, pharmaceuticals, steel, cement and biotechnology, and with even more diverse technologies. I had to grow businesses and teams from scratch as well as merge organizations and ran several change management programmes. Like many, I read books by many management gurus to find affirmation, challenge, or a new direction. At the turn of the century, I was fortunate to go through one of the best management development programmes, the *IMPM*[1]. I learnt anew under the guidance of post-modern management thinkers like Henry Mintzberg and Jonathan Gosling. I tried to apply my learning in practice and developed my own practitioner's constructs and pathways to reach our objectives. It was a great experience.

All this was required to Manage Growth.

The one thing that worked as the pivot around which any growth (change) management strategy needed to be built up was individual initiative when faced with complexity—a combination of uncertainty and opposition in varied doses. That is what I labelled as leadership for me, without which no growth was possible. Whatever as a manager I needed to do

[1] *IMPM*—The International Masters in Practising Management; www.impm.org; Cycle 6

and fulfil, I could not do it all alone. I needed at least a few others with the same individual initiative to breach the borders of certainty or agreement since across these borders lay the seeds of entry barriers or competitive advantage for an enterprise. Over the last decade, through the sessions I conducted on Leadership and Change Management at different organizations and institutions, I realized that merely exhorting others to think and behave as leaders did not create leadership. Luckily, I always met some individuals in most organizations who displayed 'individual initiative when faced with complexity' in their domains. But, this was not always created by the management. Leadership just happened.

We have good leadership only by chance, not by management. And we need to change that.

Most management thinkers like McGregor, Drucker, Koestenbaum, Handy and gurus like Mintzberg, Senge, and Kotter have rightfully emphasized on the long-term values of leadership like ethics, greatness, innovation, creativity, human depth, and social responsibility. They underscored the point that only such leadership values spawn the tenets of sustainability and growth of an organization. But the society and management has been barely dented by these exhortations. In my view, the reason for such leadership values not being nurtured consistently lies in the practice of management. Most managers make decisions and choices based on the age-old habit of 'meeting expectations', whether that of the manager or of the employee. Such expectations are normally about the short-term and out goes the long-term through the window. To deliver desired leadership values, management should instead harness the free will of individuals hooked by a long-term purpose. This book seeks to put the finger on this pressure point and pave the way for managers to live a life 'beyond expectations'.

I chose to tell my story of leadership learning and practice as a manager to my fraternity. We flit in and out of airports, check into hotels across the world, return to our homes, to our young families or ageing parents. We wake up the next morning burdened with the tasks looming in front of us. The short-term demands weigh heavily and we worry about how to make our life better. We square our shoulders for the challenges on hand, bend our heads lower on hunched shoulders, and run the risk of losing sight of the long-term. Why do we do that, why don't we look at the horizon and make today's choices? Is it something to do with the influences we grow up with? Can we avoid such apparent innocence? This book tries to answer these questions.

While the book will focus on the practice of a manager or a leader, I thought it might be interesting for readers to know a few facts about my formative years. I invite the reader for a peep into my foundation days as I believe that the choices I made and the habits of my thinking and actions as a manager were significantly influenced by the contexts I grew up with.

I grew up in Delhi in the 60s in a government colony. Delhi was definitely very safe those days, primarily a city of small-time, hard working traders and government servants with their routine, rutty lives. My family had barely enough to fulfil our basic needs, but I always knew we were special. There were three things that probably gave me this feeling of distinction as a child. My late father worked as a junior officer of the government. He was one of the few in our community who had a heavy Czech motorbike. The booming exhaust of the bike, the excited shrieks from the kids running behind it, and the surprised barking of a few pet dogs would herald his homecoming every evening. Then there was music. My mother was a delightful singer and would compose the tunes for lyrics that my father would recite—his eyes closed, lost in some reverie. The proudest moment in our lives was about us huddled together over a valve radio to listen to a live recital of the same songs by my mother on the All India Radio. Later, I too tried my hand at composing songs with my father and the experience of each successful composition was undiluted bliss. The third reason I thought we were special were the books strewn all around in our little flat. My father wrote Bengali poetry and was well versed in English literature. Most of my childhood, I heard narratives that he picked up from the writings of great statesmen, authors, and poets. India had a few statesmen in those days, not just politicians, and their speeches were worth reading and quite inspiring. While his work as an editor for the government drifted more towards the socio-political aspects, my adolescence drew me deeper into debates with him on almost any topic under the sky.

Books, debates with my father, my mother's melody, and my father's poetic wisdom and anecdotes about our ancestors who had been Sanskrit pundits probably instilled the habit to dig deeper and search for logical harmony. In my university days, I was a reluctant student of subjects taught but a voracious reader of everything beyond. After finishing my Masters in Chemistry, my academic trajectory was aimed at becoming a scientist. But, that was not to be as I could not leave my ailing father to take up a job in another city and instead became a sales guy. I learnt the ropes of selling and survival literally on the streets of Delhi in the early 80s. My first office was the armchair in my boss' living room, where we used to hatch strategies on how to generate the next order. I later joined a more respectable but staid company only to realize that I could not grow there as I was not an engineer. I left after six months to join my first professional home—an organization that matched my needs and my sense of purpose. Although my function was sales, a memorable part of that period was the training I had to give farmers in far flung rural areas to vaccinate their animals. The satisfaction lasted nine years, till I suddenly realized I was not learning anymore. I had meanwhile become a manager—recruited, developed, and managed a small team that was acknowledged for its best performance.

I was bored and work was no challenge. I decided to explore outside my company for the first time in almost ten years. That is when I met a very special person, Cherian Philip, the boss who influenced me the most. He was an entrepreneur at heart with a tremendous hunger for growth fuelled by dreams and guts. His business was a few years old in the market and represented an old German technology firm. However, it was a business I knew little about—weighing and membrane technology but basically anchored in engineering. When he asked me to join him to take over the sales responsibility, I told him that I was not an engineer—and did not want to make the same mistake as in my second job. His answer sealed my acceptance. He said, 'I am looking for a manager; you can recruit as many engineers as you want.'

I was mainly influenced by his passion in anything we discussed or got into. Initially, he took care of the financials, the operations, and charted the vision while I took care of the revenues, the people, and made sure that the business grew in the market. This was mid-90s and I was setting up my third sales team. Cherian's vision and passion made us enter into fermentation engineering on our own in India against all financial and knowledge odds. We were ridiculed, then opposed, and finally accepted by both internal as well as external forces. We had persevered and succeeded. As the business stabilized,

Cherian gradually divested his shareholding to the German principal which too had undergone dramatic changes and acquired the topmost fermentation engineering company in Europe. Subsequently, I took over the India responsibility as the manager for the Indian subsidiary. Over the next decade I went on to weave the vision and develop the Indian subsidiary into a strategic and knowledge asset of the global organization. I managed growth of people and the organization through ever increasing diversity in businesses as well as functions. It was both a challenge and a pleasure to set up two R&D units in completely diverse technology domains, engineering and production teams apart from corporate functions including Finance, HR, etc. I learnt a lot, including the value of processes, systems, tools, discipline, and commitment. But, I never allowed myself to forget that it was growth as the overarching goal that these means had to end up with.

I still run the company my boss started and he is still setting up new ventures. We used to debate a lot on why I did not want to be an entrepreneur. And my usual stand was that entrepreneurs and managers have a symbiotic existence. I have been fortunate as a manager to get the opportunity to steer the growth of a 20-man guerrilla unit into a 600-strong diverse organization with people from knowledge streams as diverse as electronics to biotechnology and mechanical engineering to microbiology. It has been an enriching journey for me—recruiting, mentoring, charting growth for different businesses and for my managers, while making myself redundant each time one of them was ready to take over a domain or an initiative. Luckily, I always found more to do but never hunted for what I should get as a consequence. I believe I grew or got different opportunities as I was just available with my capacity and capability when the context threw up an opportunity. The culture we could manage to ingrain in all we did was not to meet anyone's expectations, but to live every day 'beyond expectations'.

Like many, I have also been influenced by strong personalities who took it upon themselves to change the world they worked in: Abraham Lincoln, Swami Vivekananda, Mahatma Gandhi, Ayn Rand, Deng Xiaoping, Dr Verghese Kurien, Angela Merkel, Barack Obama, and Kiran Mazumdar Shaw are a few such names I can cite easily. It is their individuality that inspires me and the responsibility they took to stand up for themselves, their convictions, and their vision. As a 20-year-old, I discovered Ayn Rand and her objectivist philosophy celebrating selfishness as a virtue. Her philosophy pulled me like a magnet, particularly the exalted position she accorded to the individual. It was only much later in life that I defined selfishness to myself as the onus to develop your own self. The Germans have a nice word for that—*bildung*. The entire Indian philosophy drawn from ancient Hindu epics is based upon the concept of *aham brahma,* not interpreted as 'I am God', but in 'I have potential to find all greatness in me!'. Drawing upon such precepts, if managers can at least take the onus on their shoulders to develop themselves, one would not get controlled by motivators but one's own guiding purpose and vision.

Introduction

> *'Unless the distant goals of meaning, greatness, and destiny are addressed, we can't make an intelligent decision about what to do tomorrow morning—much less set strategy for a company or for a human life. Nothing is more practical than for people to deepen themselves. The more you understand the human condition, the more effective you are as a businessperson. Human depth makes (even) business sense.'*[2]
>
> PETER KOESTENBAUM

This book is for individuals who would like to end their lives with a smile on their lips reminiscing about what they have left behind in the minds and lives of other people. The 'beyond expectations' way offers an alternative approach to management, or even life in general. It may help wean people away from being mainly driven by the *natural* expectation of gratifying unfulfilled needs—the 'meeting expectations' way of motivation explained by Abraham Maslow in 1943. The morass we see in organizations or the society today, the consistent compromise of values, the stressed and cynical faces we see in mirrors or

[2] Koestenbaum, P., (2002), Interview on Leadership reported in 'Fast Company', 2002

otherwise, the busy manager and the shackled employee—are all sicknesses with aetiologies rooted in the unbridled practice of motivation theory aimed at the lower needs of mankind. The 'meeting expectations' way stokes the short-term approach in man resulting in a self-created predatory society, dragging us into the nadirs of a lowest common denominator (LCD) Syndrome. The LCD Syndrome and how we unknowingly create a predatory society is explained in Part 2.

I propose instead a long-term, purpose-driven leadership grounded in volitional engagement to wrench us out of this malaise. This book seeks to usher readers out of the motivational trap, actualize their development potential that most of us are naturally bestowed with, and become Leader Managers. This book is about Growth Management, as it is leader managers who create growth and none else.

Leader managers are people who decide and act driven by the Purpose of Action and not by what they may make in the bargain. These leaders are not caged by others' or their own expectations. They are able to contribute to leadership values like ethics, empathy, creativity, innovation, greatness, social responsibility, and development of other conscientious leaders. This leads to Remarkable Achievements and the final goal of an enterprise—sustained profitable growth. There cannot be anything more remarkable than the above leadership values that one may wish from managers or management who steer enterprises (public and private) and indirectly the society we live in.

As a practising manager, I have been lucky to be mostly in the business of growth management. This purpose brought me to an obsessive search for what—if not short-term pecuniary motivators—makes leaders contribute towards remarkable achievements. Remarkable, as they had to be achieved in situations laced with uncertainty, ambiguity, opposition, or lack of agreement—characterized by the word, complexity.

I found a simple link between growth management and leadership, which I present below as the practising manager's growth mantra.

The Practising Manager's Growth Mantra

- Growth in an enterprise is created through remarkable achievements, not incremental achievements like efficiency or effectiveness.
- Remarkable achievements are possible only in complexity.
- Only volitional engagement can work in complexity. Luckily, there is no certainty in complexity. Hence, motivational engagement cannot work.
- People who make choices based on the purpose can only be volitionally engaged—they are the growth managers, the leaders.

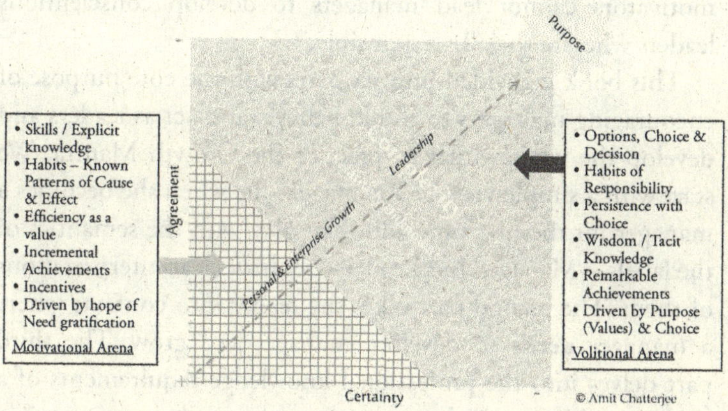

FIG. 1 – THE PRACTISING MANAGER'S GROWTH MANTRA

The link between remarkable achievements, complexity, and leadership lies so close to the borders of anarchy or utopia that only finite mindsets based upon choice and volition can provide deeper anchoring. Uncertainty, temptation, risk, attrition, globalization, multiple cultures, and varying contexts need sustained leadership based on sustainable leadership values. And this cannot come from fragile motivational engagement that can be blown away by winds of uncertainty or opposition. While motivation theory, systems, and processes are necessary for executing day-to-day operations, these are not helpful in developing foresight, building strategies, differentiation, or in developing leaders who can manage all the above with sustained quality and ownership.

Motivation theory as practiced in organizations is mostly about pecuniary benefits that offer a reasonable hope of gratifying baser needs like survival or self-esteem. These motivators may lead to incremental achievements, but not to remarkable achievements or develop leadership values like ethics, empathy, creativity, innovation, or greatness. Short-term motivators cannot lead managers to develop conscientious leaders who are socially responsible.

This book is divided into six parts with the core purpose of encouraging managers to think, believe, and act as leaders and develop the wherewithal to practice the Growth Mantra. We start with a simple view of a manager's life when she becomes a manager for the first time and then play with the semantics of the labels—Manager and Leader—to draw clear interpretations of them. The second part takes the reader into contexts where a manager needs to develop, manage, and grow. The third part delves into the professional knowledge requirements of a manager without which one can be, at best, a layman manager. In the fourth part, we see the manager in practice as a leader and find application of the Growth Mantra. The fifth part explains the evolution of a leader and pegs the onus of developing leadership on parenting, managers, and the individual before probing deeper into Growth Management in today's global business environment.

Every chapter is a real-life expression or experience of a practising manager. The reader goes through a roller-coaster ride of sometimes thinking as a manager, at other times as a leader or a follower. Each paradigm under discussion gives you a chance to reflect and cross your own Rubicons[3] into the world of volition or remain a prisoner of volatile motivators, whether intrinsic or extrinsic. The last part is a first person account of the vulnerability in decision making and the various choices with changing contexts and quandary in the life of a manager—resulting in reflections on life as a whole. After all, the work of a manager or a leader is just a subset of her entire life.

In sharing my little journey, I sincerely hope that 'The Practising Manager's Growth Mantra' provokes readers and helps knowledge workers and managers in choosing a way forward that leads to happiness, actualization of their potential, and bring back the romance of an enterprise in the knowledge industry and society we live in today.

---

[3] The Rubicon Model is referred to in the chapter, 'The Volition Arena'

PART 1

The Semantics of Managerial identity

This part seeks to draw sharp contours around the labels, the 'Manager' and the 'Leader'. The purpose is to use these labels to qualify contexts and roles that individuals have to play in organizations as well as society at large. We will go into these polarities of the managerial role and have some fun being a manager or a leader…or both!

- *'The Manager' relates to the realization of becoming a manager.*
- *The 'Manager–Leader Divide' instigates a debate in the reader's mind that may help in making a clear choice of wanting to be a leader or not.*
- *'Developing Leaders' paints the paradox that leads to the cognition of the need for leadership and the dilemma in managing consequences.*

Those who practiced the Growth Mantra knowingly or unknowingly, succeeded in avoiding the paradox or the pains of a dilemma.

1

The Manager

Nobody told me that I would one day be referred to as a Manager. Nobody told me that to be a manager could be a career objective. Many years after having the word 'manager' as a part of my job title, I started to warm up to the word consciously. It took some more years to feel secure enough to consciously utter the self-introduction—'I am a Manager'.

While I was getting used to the label manager, another label cropped up repeatedly to be consistently debated internally and externally. And this one was not a new one; the debate was being or not, a leader! Although, it is true that leadership is required at every level of an organization, the person referred to, accused of, or exhorted to be a leader is normally one who has already earned the title of a manager. I am not going to debate the question, whether a manager is a leader, should be, could be, has to be, or not. The answer for all that probably lies in the exponential proliferation of books, academic work, gurus, workshops, power talkers, changes in the OB curriculum, etc. with the words manage(r)ment and leadership.

It is not just fashion that the last couple of decades have seen the word *leadership* creep more and more into the organizational arena and cosy up to the older inhabitant, *strategy*. Strategy probably came to roost at the same time as Peter Drucker discovered the *knowledge worker*. Strategy has something to do with leadership. I will discuss that relationship later. What I find intriguing about the advent of the leadership phenomenon is that the label leader has been used, lauded and emulated, and dropped like a hot potato—all in tandem in discussions about managers—whether in the real workplace or in the academic domain. The society at large has accepted the label of manager, but is yet to make peace with the label of a leader. This probably has something to do with the uneasiness the label leader causes to not only the self, but anyone around the person who may get stuck with the label. It is often a label that most aspire for, work hard to be acknowledged for, but always feel or are made to feel uncomfortable with, when used too often in either first person or third.

The manager–leader paradox appears to me to be more of an identity crisis of the Jekyl and Hyde genre. And not surprisingly again, the leader is perceived to be the difficult guy whereas the manager is comparatively the good guy. And that is probably why no organization has dared to label a role or box in the organogram as *Dy. Leader–Manufacturing or General Leader–Marketing*. We all snuggle into the relative warmth of the label manager when given the choice between being a leader or a manager. Hence, let me also shy away for some time from the label leader and dwell on the label manager.

What Are the Good Things Associated with the Label Manager?

In most cases, a celebration is the norm when someone from the trenches gets promoted as a manager. The spouse expects a gift or plans a feast when the partner becomes a senior manager.

Peers, bosses, business associates congratulate heartily and promptly when they hear of your new position as a big manager. The salary increase, the corner office, the bigger company car, expense account, fancier gadgets, flashy new business card, even a new chair and an assistant are all accoutrements that beget the congratulations, accolades, and celebrations.

Even you celebrate with some justified sense of entitlement and gift yourself a new business suit, a more expensive watch, an appropriate briefcase, a white-starred piece of stationery, and what not. On the family front, you start planning the next acquisition, be it a new kitchen accessory, furniture, drapes, bed, a pet, or even a new flat or a bigger house. Children are sent off to higher cost or more reputed schools and if you are lucky enough to be yet connected to your parents, you indulge them with a vacation or a heart-warming gift. The large hearted even regale the secretary with something she can boast of having got from the boss, the manager, or is it the leader?

Anyhow, all the above positives of becoming a manager relate to the *what*—what an individual achieved or got on becoming a manager. Finally, all celebrations have to end and all the congratulations ebb away to pave the way for the manager to *start managing*. This is when all the positives of becoming a manager have already become digested, including the salary raise.

The manager's job takes over and what is that? It is not remotely related to what it was in the trenches or whatever she had to do earlier. It is different. More often than not, she is not even trained to do what the job entails. The expertise that was thought to have earned her the promotion is not what she can use anymore. Former comrades in arms in the trenches keep working the same way but the brand new manager is not required to do that anymore.

- The manager is required to plan and monitor what needs to be done in the trenches—that is not so difficult.
- The manager maybe required to train the trenchers on what, how, or when has to be done—even that is not so difficult.
- The manager is required to understand what kind of mindset is required by the people who have to work in the trenches, select correct attitudes and habits as individuals and keep them motivated—that sounds so interesting—but the manager has no training to do these things.
- The manager is expected to resolve conflicts between different people in her team as well as between other stakeholder functions.

I was supposed to study hard, get a job, do my trench job well, and get promoted. I achieved all that, only to wallow in this pit of human conflicts! Why did I study engineering or biochemistry? This should involve a psychotherapist or a behavioural scientist!

2

The Manager—Leader Divide

'The only consistent constituent in any growth strategy is change. Success comes from people who are motivated by the change, not from those who need to be motivated to change. Does it matter who conceived the strategy, the purpose to change?'

Most definitions about a manager's role still leads to one of the oldest and the shortest, that of *'Predicting and and Controlling Results'.* Managers are expected to predict and control the results of the short-term, be it a quarter or a year, and then what? No farther? Nobody dares to spell it out.

Is this because one does not expect the manager to be there to manage a longer term or they themselves are asked by their management to only deliver the short-term. Is the top management clear about whether to clarify this question or do they live this as a dilemma? I believe this lack of clarity or dilemma is what leads to the Manager –Leader Divide. Managers are mostly employees, paid a monthly wage, an annual increment, and reviewed for performance (annually in innocent organizations or quarterly in the insane ones). The employer or their representative, the management is obviously there to ensure the returns on costs and hence, treats the manager as a machine that has to keep chugging at the most efficient rate. How can we expect leadership values of the long-term when the management or assessment culture in enterprises is based on the shortest tenure?

Let us test the waters of managerial or leadership development in organizations. While it is quite normal to see countless initiatives in organizations for developing good managers, it is not abnormal to hear of a few programmes for leadership development too. But, the stats appear to be heavily in favour of managerial trainings rather than that for leadership development—probably because it is easier to develop managerial *skills* as opposed to leadership *wisdom*. As I have the luxury of not being an academic, I can wager that most enterprises spend resources on managerial vs. leadership development in the range of 90:10 across any one industry. Take it as a provocation if you wish since I would be very happy to be proven wrong by miles. Please note that the label 'managerial' has been used for company initiatives/trainings on managing 'inanimate' topics, while the label 'leadership' has been used for competence or knowledge required for managing 'animate(d)' subjects.

Thankfully, the universe around always plays the balancing act. In this context, we have seen the mushrooming of book shops, reading parlours, power talkers, leadership seminars, etc. around the enterprise world, endeavouring to balance the skewed focus inside enterprises against leadership development. Even the traditional MBA programmes around the world are revamping the curriculum by adding more and more leadership electives in a hurry. New leadership institutions pop up every other day in different parts of the world hoping to somehow stem the rot in leadership manifestation in organizations and society at large. Over the last decade, airport book shops have relegated books on managerial issues like TQM, Quality, Project management to remote corners, while books on leadership hog the limelight overflowing prime space.

> *It does appear that enterprises and their managers are incapable of developing leadership, and somehow make ends meet through developing managers. It is like living on black coffee and packed food, since I never learnt to cook the tasty traditional dishes of my childhood.*

Let me use business process to drive the wedge deeper into the manager–leader divide. Broadly thinking, the business process is about two major sub-processes. The first is about all things that 'grows business', like customer orientation, product development, process innovation, market strategy, succession development, risk decisions, to name a few. The other sub-process is about all that 'execute business'. These are most of the daily tasks that any organization needs to perform with the best of efficiency and effectiveness. These are simple tasks as qualified in the Stacey's Matrix (Fig. 2) and engages the major part of the organization's resources. Tasks that grow business need manifestation of leadership, while those that execute business need the appropriate engagement of a manager. Leadership tasks require an ability to *en-vision* the future (even for an individual role) and execute the entire change management process that would create business for times to come. Managerial tasks, on the other hand, need deep involvement to ensure the most effective and efficient execution of all that has been decided. Yes, I am playing with semantics!

Envisioning and change management by a leader requires a long-term engagement and comfort with uncertainty—integral to leadership thinking and action. On the other hand, execution by a manager normally needs a comparatively shorter term focus and a passion for the tiniest of incremental improvements. These tendencies are normally the forte of experts or routine taskmasters, not common in visionaries or strategists. However, beware of the temptation to accept the corollary that all visionaries or strategists would be good leaders.

Leaders are passionate about the purpose, while Managers need to be passionate about the results. Thankfully, the world does produce exceptions as a combination of leadership and managerial mettle. They are the managers who contribute to sustained profitable growth in any organization.

The Leader Unleashes Remarkable Achievement

The manager sits on the relatively simpler side of the river named Complexity. Complexity in this book is characterized as defined in Ralph Stacey's *Matrix of Certainty and Agreement*[4]. Once a manager wets her toes in these waters, she develops the taste to embrace complexity and learn to invest in it. You are swimming in waters of Complexity when one needs to work out decisions and actions where the stakeholders are not in agreement nor are you certain about what or how things got to be done. It is in these waters the Manager transforms into a Leader or simply perishes.

Jumping into the river of complexity is like crossing the Rubicon, the river Julius Caesar decided to cross with his legions in 49 BC to regain Rome. On one side of the river named Complexity lies the normal life of a manager, dealing with politics, diplomacy, domain knowledge, linear logic, root

---

4 Stacey, R, (1996), 'Complexity and Creativity in Organizations', (Berrett-Koehler, 1996). More details on p. 161.

cause driven causation planning and achievement. They are not exactly simple tasks. Stacey calls them complicated tasks made of unknowns to the uninitiated, but knowable to those with appropriate managerial skills and experience. On the other side of the divide lies the sea of complexity—teeming with uncertainty, lack of agreement, conflicts and potential for growth creation. This is where leadership is nurtured and needs to flourish. Once Complexity is breached, growth ensues, Rome will be regained and thereafter starts afresh the Manager's life, that of business execution or running Rome!

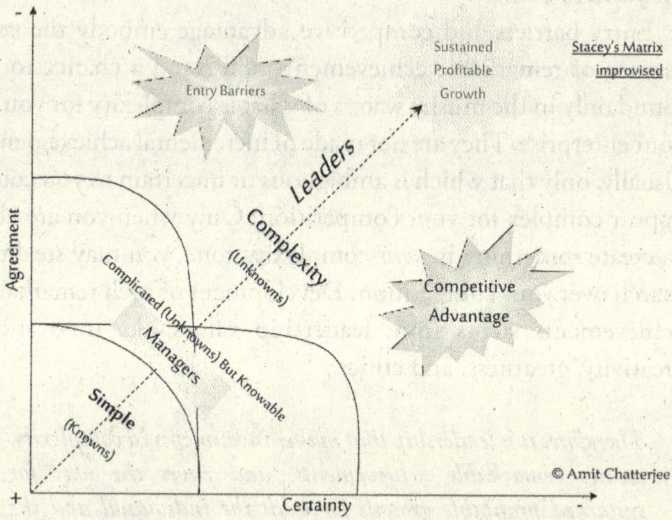

Simple & Complicated decisions are being made every day by our Competitors, Customers & Us. Decisions and Investments in the Complex Zone could be the way out for Sustained Profitable Growth

FIG. 2 – STACEY'S MATRIX AND GROWTH MANAGEMENT

I have used the Stacey's Matrix to develop a construct for Growth Management. It shows the relationship between investment in complexity and the long-term objective of any enterprise—sustained profitable growth (SPG). The logic is very simple—to achieve SPG, an enterprise has to keep developing *entry barriers* and *competitive advantage*. Now, such buzzwords are clearly not about simple tasks where past patterns or pathways are efficiently and effectively executed. Nor are they about complicated tasks where a manager's expertise or experience can get the job done. Simple and complicated tasks are doable by your competition as well as they also employ skilled managers. Incremental achievements in simple and complicated tasks may keep the business in the race for the short-term, but would not be enough to maintain sustainability or continued profitability for years to come.

Entry barriers and competitive advantage embody the very essence of remarkable achievements and stand a chance to be found only in the mushy waters of what is complexity for you or your enterprise. They are not made of incremental achievements. Usually, only that which is ambiguous or uncertain to you could appear complex for your competition. Only when you are able to create something in *your* complexity zone, you may steal the march over your competition. Development of such remarkable achievements stems from leadership values like innovation, creativity, greatness, and ethics.

> *Therefore, it is leadership that makes investments in complexity, creates remarkable achievements, and paves the way for sustained profitable growth for both the individual and the organization.*

The Leader–Manager Divide Continues

The divide gets accentuated in growing organizations where a communication deficit develops between managers in leader mode and those in manager mode. The leader-mode managers are busy fishing in complexity—thinking how to 'transform Rome'—while those in manager mode are expected to be studiously 'running Rome'. More often than not, the leader-mode managers tend to be bosses to those in manager mode and as they are in one organization, the managers do have something to do with their leader-mode bosses while running Rome.

The bosses, while busy crunching complexity—decisions and actions for building the future of the same organization, running investigations and analysis to find certainty in uncertain waters, or politicking with diplomacy to bring differing and different people on board to cement agreement—at times forget their managerial duties in managing the managers running Rome. It is undoubtedly a difficult ask. Crunching complexity is not only taxing on your mental time, but also intoxicating. For most, if not all, it feeds into their narcissistic needs quite sumptuously.

The managers running Rome at times are left high and dry looking for directions or decisions for their Rome running tasks as they may not have authority for all the decisions that they need to make. In such cases, they have no alternative but to either wait or postpone actions while their leader managers are busy with their priorities from crunching complexity. This is when the divide becomes even wider and the organization, today's Rome, begins to show signs of malfunctioning. It does help if the leader managers plan and devote time periodically for their management tasks while those in manager mode learn to demand clarifications and decisions for their Rome running responsibilities.

I painted the above divide in an organizational context. One may apply the above by keeping the onus entirely on oneself as well. We all as managers have the possibility to choose leader-mode activities which would mean investing our faculties in what is complex for us in our individual context and role in the organization. On the other hand for smooth functioning, we should have our manager-mode tasks or duties chalked out clearly.

> *And lest one forgets, you are also a leader manager to your subordinates. Without some bits of complexity in your domain, you are just a manager. With only complexity, you are not a manager at all.*

Where Leadership Begins

One of the most interesting questions about Leadership could be, Just as a manager is assigned the task of running Rome or to execute daily business, can a leader be assigned the task to grow the business or transform Rome? Then comes the next question—Who assigns such a challenging task? Is this a manager in leader mode or in manager mode? How does the impact vary and why?

While you ponder on these questions, let me veer off a bit into some rougher terrains:

- *Why should 'Rome' be transformed at all? Can't we achieve the long-term organizational goal of SPG without changing the status quo?*
- *What should the status-quo be changed into? Who is expected to be thinking of such a question? Would it be a manager in leader mode or in manager mode?*
- *What is the precursor to change management? If it is vision for the future, shouldn't the vision (as opposed to the visionary) drive change management? Who needs to build and explain the vision to others in the organization?*
- *Can you motivate a person to have a vision for a company, a division, or a team? Can expectations of gratifying unfulfilled needs motivate a manager to develop people,*

create innovation, work towards greatness, or be ethical?

- *Is it possible for an enterprise to achieve SPG, if the top manager or management only has leadership capabilities?*
- *Do we need vision and change execution for the next hierarchical levels, such as that for a division, a department, or a team?*

The answers to the questions above are obvious to most in the organizational world. Hence, I leave that to my readers' context, experience, and wisdom. The challenge does not lie in knowing the right answers but in the gap between knowledge and action. We know that we need to have a distant vision for our responsibilities and life in general. We know this distant vision should tell us what choices to make today and not be motivated by short-term gratifications. And being driven by the distant goals is leadership manifested. Short-term motivators can only fulfil short-term goals and they may not coalesce into a pathway towards our distant vision. Then why do most of us stray and at best try to be good short-term managers. While doing that we influence others around us too to live or work for short-term gratifications. We thus create the morass we complain about in our society. Why? Why we behave as mere managers and not leaders when we have the knowledge to know what is right? The individual's insecurity in managing the long-term, the uncertainties of the future makes us desire the fulfilment of all needs, wants, and dreams in the shortest term. A way out is to spread these aspirational gaps over a timeline. Needs being such things that need be fulfilled at the earliest, while wants could be gratified over the mid term and dreams after reaching certain future milestones.

Managers who ask or assign leadership tasks for others, if not driven by distant visions will fail to create leadership in their organizations. The onus of leadership development squarely lies on the management in the organizational context while every individual carries the potential of leadership thinking. The management is responsible for creating the culture that would nurture leaders at all levels to envision change for growth in their own domains. One way to initiate this culture is to *believe in and expect* leadership behaviour from others and not look upon you only as the leader.

> *Else, very soon, the captains will be forced to come and run the engines below the deck. No shippie who has risen to the captain's cabin wants to dirty his hands again with engine oil or spanners. Captains, beware! Leadership begins at home.*

3

Developing Leaders—Paradox or a Dilemma?

Who will take up the task of developing leaders?
Who has the time for it and the habits to do it?
Are these questions asked by managers or an enterprise's management every week, if not every day?

Leadership in the society or in business has probably hit the most complex morass due to the past being of not much help in tackling the challenges of today or unravelling the mysteries of tomorrow. The past is helpful for those contexts that have not changed but most contexts have changed and are changing almost at the same pace as the pages of an old-fashioned printed calendar. Ironically, the larger part of the management world and managers remain too busy with objectives perched atop their nose-tips or mostly focussed on training managers for their *skills*. No wonder as it is the skills that gets the job done on a daily level or that required for executing business. Leadership *wisdom* is normally relegated to the back burner for being too mushy, too slow for quarterly or even annual ROIs. It is true that management is not so good at tackling beyond the nose-tip itch. That is probably why the topic of leadership starts with a paradox and slips into the waters of dilemma in most organizations.

The Paradox

Tons of management literature and weeks of discussions are dedicated to the need for leaders and developing leadership, but not much is said about selecting leaders. Organizations recruit college graduates, experts, or managers to fill up positions that are defined to do the tasks of the day or for running Rome. They normally do not recruit leaders knowingly. Later, in situations that demand leadership thinking and actions, managers or management lament the paucity of leadership talent or potential in their organizations. Hence the resulting paradox. We do not knowingly recruit leaders but expect them to think, decide, and act as leaders when we realize the need for leadership thinking and action.

The Dilemma Begins

The realization of the shortage of leadership, when needed, gives rise to the dilemma for the management. More often than not this realization is a bit late in the day as it is no longer possible to develop leaders inside the organization for the positions or context that need leadership qualities. The dilemma sets in—to bring in managers for leadership positions from outside the organization or not.

Such positions normally need leadership talent as these are pivotal roles and not for routine tasks. Change management is one of the most important requirements from such leadership positions. Most managements are conscious of the risks in bringing in outsiders, but are left with little choice as the gaps are normally for relatively senior positions and need to be filled up immediately. Sadly, such leadership-scarce organizations end up filling these gaps with a majority coming from outside the organization or as compromises from the best possible insiders.

In case of outsiders, even if the choice has been good enough, the incumbent could lack something precious. It could be the lack of 'emotional connect' to the organization or the challenges on hand or the lack of empathy with the rest of the organization. The worst could come true if the choice ended up with a narcissist who wears the facade of a leader. In the managerial world, a narcissist by definition is one who pursues relentlessly such goals that could fulfil his need for fame and power and not necessarily the purpose of the organization. A narcissist is the archaic senior manager who is perennially in the domain of motivation, driven by what he will personally gain and not the organizational goals. The organizational objectives are the means to achieve his narcissistic ends. Such people would immediately press the eject button once they perceive any threat to their potential for fame or power.

Hence, before we bemoan the lack of leadership, we need to sow the seeds of leadership.

The Panacea

Managers or management need to have enough distant vision to envisage the need for leadership at multiple levels and roles in the organization. This distant vision is what generates a strong commitment to the process and details of developing leadership. This process makes the manager think beyond the inanimate aspects of the domain the manager manages. It is definitely not about meeting expectations, rather it starts with thinking beyond. A wish or a habit to imagine a distant vision for your domain of responsibility is what makes the mind to think beyond the daily grind. Conjuring up in your mind what the current context should transform into in 'n' number of years sets the blood gushing through your veins. Anxiety for how to make that vision possible makes the adrenaline pour and you transform from a manager into a leader as you are thinking about what it should be in some years and not how it has to be by the end of the quarter. You are now the captain of a ship that is on a voyage instead of a trapeze artist who performs the same task everyday with no errors. You are charting the future for your organization, your team, and of course for yourself too but as a leader not for your own narrow personal gain. You are respected, looked up to, and even followed. You are in the business of transforming Rome or creating growth.

The growth trajectory of the current context matures in your mind every day and every minute. All who work with you see you working for the organization's growth and that inspires them too to develop and eventually grow. They feel the onus on themselves to learn and invest in themselves and also align their knowledge with the future requirements for growth. They start thinking, deciding, and acting based on where they have to reach and not yearn for short-term motivators only. Everybody including you is now exploring what all can be done today that will create the envisaged tomorrow. The daily tasks are done with gusto not needing any motivational batons or carrots as people feel that the daily tasks are the means to reach the future goals. It is no more a grind but a given that has to be done the best way, efficiently and effectively, as these are the early steps of the ladder leading to the wanted future. People do things wilfully and not because they are enticed to do it. Leadership as a culture wafts all across pervading each mind and each activity with a sense of purpose. Growth is the purpose and when people work for their future, they create energy not consume it. Not only revenues are brought forward as the growth virus reigns supreme, even costs get reduced as efficiencies pile up. One can hear the whirr of several growth engines buzzing everywhere. Leadership thinking, actions, and values abound all across and the management is egged on to think even bigger and finds it easier to decide on more investments as they feel convinced about the resources. Animate and animated resources crunch inanimate complications or challenges in their stride and the organization bursts at its seams with fun and energy as the ship toots ahead on its way towards sustained profitable growth!

That is the spirit of a growth organization nurtured by managers who have developed the habits of developing leaders and do not need to be tasked for creating growth. But, before we start celebrating the euphoric spirit, one needs to get drenched in the managerial context and science. The next two parts will address these two important tenets of management 'technology' which could be helpful to mitigate the risk of becoming a layman manager—one who lacks the professional knowledge of managing people. The following pages are a bold attempt at an insight into this technology domain.

PART 2

The Manager's Premise

The Manager's Premise makes one pause and examine the kind of organizational and societal situation one has to work in. It helps the reader to put her or his finger on issues that could be the causation for the malaise we as managers have to straddle, both on the organizational and the individual plane. The chapters leave you with some questions and choices that could lead you, your organization, and by default the society into a happier place to live and work in.

- *The 'Barons and the Knowledge Workers' paints a provocative picture about the evolution of the business enterprise, where shareholder barons succeeded in subverting the knowledge society to their greed by using pecuniary benefits as the only measure for success. Managers are the lead knowledge workers. They are the only class of leaders who can lead a way out of this morass! (Exceptions to the rule obviously exist only to warn us of what could go wrong.)*
- *The next chapter explores the etiology behind the deterioration of human society into a Lowest Common Denominator (LCD) Syndrome, where most find it convenient to compromise and settle with 'satisfactory underperformance'. This piece ends with a suggestion to escape from this syndrome.*
- *'Making a Point' is a simple investigation into the more prevalent individual mindset we come across in organizations and society, where one suffers from this overarching need to make a point to all around us. This*

leads to conflicts at every stage of work or life. Managers have to deal with such behaviour each day. This chapter could help the reader to tackle such situations and most importantly use the understanding to prevent the propagation of a predatory society.

1

The Barons and the Knowledge Workers

If man was supposed to be a first among equals, the utopia must not have lasted long. Since he learnt to grow his food, he learnt the value of maintaining an asset—be it the land where he grew the food or the food itself that needed to be stored and traded. Ownership of property became the currency for survival and later, supremacy. As currency became the next asset in a seemingly civilized world, capital joined property to destroy any chances for the utopia of equality to grow roots. Many a battle was fought and a lot of blood was shed before a few cemented their roost wielding their sons, sticks, and guns to become the zamindars (landlords in India) or barons of capital and property.

Agriculture gave rise to the need for implements and tools. Storage of surplus food and the landlords' need for trading probably ushered in the dramatic developments in modes of transportation. Society became divided between the landed and the landless. In India, the landed and the powerful became the Maharajas with their private armies. Craftsmen burgeoned all over the world, busy meeting the demands of a mercantile civilization yet backed largely by an agricultural economy. They were probably the first 'knowledge workers' with their honed skills and continuous innovations in the fast expanding economic landscape of humanity. Yet, a craftsman's 'knowledge' was not enough to make him too valuable or wealthy as the skills required could be trained in as many apprenticed under the masters to meet the ever growing demand for their craft. Property and wealth remained the major entry barriers to protect the supremacy of the landed.

With the onset of industrialization in Europe, the barons of capital and property were better placed to leverage their assets and network to emerge as owners of manufacturing businesses. Capitalism found its identity on one end of the industrial divide as wealth could fund machines, employ workers, and finance trade. The barons had it all to rule the society; they became the neo-royalty with their fast growing industrial empires, creating worker jobs for the multitudes of landless. For the first time, society tasted fruits of economic development. Demands of industrialization gave rise to the polytechnic or technical universities in Europe in the 19th century and later in the US and those born 'good and poor' found knowledge as their only way to a better life.

At the same time, nation states replaced kingdoms; battles became wars fought with more and more sophisticated and devastating weaponry. Businesses grew faster during war times and the former barons of capital and property became the owners of ever growing large industrial fiefdoms. Post World War II, technology surfaced as the major entry barrier financially owned by industrial barons but more and more intellectually owned by the employee. The barons ruled supreme till technology became too complex to be acquired through wealth alone. Knowledge spread faster among the working class as they outnumbered the progenies of the landed and gradually became the differentiator between competing enterprises instead of capital. This was what made Peter Drucker coin the phrase 'Knowledge Worker' in the 60s in the US. He argued that 'Knowledge has become the key resource that knows no geography and went on to state that every knowledge worker in a modern organization is an "executive" by virtue of his position or knowledge'.

Industrialization and later globalization heralded the ascent of the knowledge worker (KW) and since then, they have been threatening the old forts of barons of capital and property. The KW became the managers and executives of an enterprise owned by the modern day barons, the shareholders. These managers became responsible for contributions that materially influenced the capacity of an organization to perform and create results. The shareholder barons could no longer directly manage their large enterprises, nor could they possess all the varied knowledge required to run the industries of the day. Fast changing markets and technologies raised their dependency on the KW Managers. On the other hand, the KWs needed the barons to earn value for their knowledge and also develop their knowledge as it is the enterprise as a context where the knowledge of the KW gets developed as well as valued. Knowledge became the major ingredient for the strategy of an enterprise. The barons realized that they could not treat the KW as just a wage-earning manual worker. They had earlier mastered the art of managing the manual worker by gratifying their basic needs like food and shelter, but the knowledge worker was a different proposition. He has higher needs and even dreams to fulfil. The barons were in search for the right lever to control these knowledge workers.

The divide between the KWs and the shareholder barons had to be bridged. What evolved was the top management team led by the top knowledge worker as the CEO. The barons knew that the middle management layer would always be ready to snap at any opportunity in case the top management failed.

They could now afford to dignify and edify the best knowledge worker as the CEO while discarding him as a scapegoat in times of upheavals or turmoil knowing there would be another sucker in the wings somewhere. In this complex tug of war between the shareholder barons and the CEO, the only tangibles that they could believe in to be used as a buoy or a measure to keep him on leash, were pecuniary benefits. CEOs came to be motivated or controlled only in terms of financial results, compensations, perks, club memberships, paid holidays, bonuses, stock options, share price, and so on. The celebrated knowledge worker, one of the finer specimens of the human race and their conclaves as organizations, became reduced to commodities weighed in terms of numbers only. Success became synonymous with net worth, credit cards, or the model of cars one drove in. Well, quite logical as intangible parameters like greatness, creativity, innovation, ethics, human values, or social responsibility are very difficult to measure at least in the short-term. Long-term was too long for shareholder barons to stake their investments on the KWs whom they could never trust much anyway.

As knowledge spread faster and business organizations, models, and processes became more and more complex, sometimes beyond the comprehension of the barons, the same CEOs or 'top management' became the *frankensteins* haunting the shareholder barons by pushing them with their backs to the wall. Either the barons lost control over these KW CEOs or were rendered clueless at incidences of rampant financial irregularities. They sought succour in regulatory- or statutory-powers-to-be only to find them going in cahoots with the new monarchs of the organizations—the CEOs. Top management greed, corruption of government bureaucrats and politicians facilitated by statutory audit firms are daily fodder for the business news industry across the world.

They say, what cannot be measured does not count. So, why try to measure those vague intangibles? Since the CEOs were measured or assessed only by financial results, they used the same reward-systems to steer their subordinates. One of my co-workers and friend once said, 'All men are born good and poor (relatively)'. If my friend was right, then the same should hold good for most KWs too. The barons promoted the same KWs as CEOs and due to a lack of trust or not wanting to risk what they possessed started using pecuniary benefits as a carrot and a stick since they could not see beyond their noses.

Alas! The outcome has been devastating. The fine specimens of humanity, after being forced into habits of gratification from pecuniary benefits alone, got relegated to living just for comparative supremacy. Exalted pursuits like leadership values evaporated into misty domains of professorial literature. The ungratified need for more and more money and whatever that could buy became the only motivators, leaving the poor, vague intangibles behind. The misty higher needs as per Maslow's need hierarchy gathered dust in library racks to be sometimes glorified at temples of passive intellectuality.

The KWs who were born good and relatively poor with aspirations to grow up into fine specimens of the human race, nurtured by their doting middle-class parents, degenerated into CEOs who would wield the same motivational baton that they were being beaten with. The shareholder barons had their last laugh. They had succeeded with the last trick that every imperial colonizer had applied in the 20th century. The KWs with their dreams and aspirations were caged, tamed, whipped into roaring freely at the lash of a whip from their employers. They were given their pound of flesh only after they had danced to the tune of their shareholder masters. We hear of top management stress and burnouts, and even those stress management workshops and medical bills for the burning CEOs that are paid for by shareholder funds like a circus lion is given free–of–charge veterinary care.

The biggest irony is that even these shareholder barons or their predecessors were also born good and poor. The worst fallout is that these KW CEOs who were born good and poor are today castigated by those who loved them, nurtured them, as they have today become the neo-shareholder barons. And the motivational baton passes on, down the line across most levels and functions of most organizations.

Yes, it is catch-22, densely populated in most organizations, individual lives, teams, divisions, decision-making, evaluations, and promotions, everywhere. KWs like tamed circus lions are ending up doing less than what they are essentially asked to do on a result level and like the kings of the wild in a circus ring are not doing everything out of their free will but to gratify some basic needs of food, shelter, security, and comparative survival.

Well; is that what the Knowledge Workers in our society should end up as?

Tamed, tied to the aprons of the shareholder trainers, trying to live up to their expectations, never being able to meet the insatiable hunger for more as most shareholders logically are there for the ROI. Hence, the KW ends up in a 'satisfactory underperformance' loop, always being told that you are not that good after all as you are not able to meet our expectations always. The KW had grown up acquiring knowledge, creating knowledge, and using knowledge. Battling in the pits of shareholder value creation, these good habits got whittled away in the beginning and finally the remnants were ripped away or torched away by the scorching heat of, well, money.

The new habits required to be developed to survive in these modern day roman pits were antithetical to the very teachings the KW had received all her life and contrary to what she was teaching her children, if she had the time and tenacity to have them! That is where the top-management stress comes from; psychological wrenching that asks their conscious to ignore or not recognize what their subconscious cannot throw away as precious.

- Is that what the doting parents wished their loving wards to grow up into?
- Is that what we have to work hard for?
- Is that what our children should end up with?
- Is that what all our Knowledge, Intelligence, and Diligence can come up with?

Questions galore. It has become fashionable not to answer such questions and when you do not do something for some time, not doing it becomes a habit, goes out of fashion, and our self-evaluation metrics. Is there a way out of this industry *colosseum*, where the gloating shareholders in the galleries are only interested in the share price going up or at best the dividend warrants after the show ends for the day?

Yes! The way out is not to be driven by the motivational baton, but to be pulled by a Goal. Strive for the objectives and values one believes in, can commit to, and enjoy to work for. The way out is to harness and fuel the volitional energies of individuals and not offer them carrots for achieving the purpose. The way out is to clarify the purpose of working in an enterprise and use it as the beacon for the journey. The way out is to work for sustainability of the enterprise, value for the buyers of what the enterprise creates, and actualization of the development potential of the people who work for the enterprise.

Working towards fulfilling the expectations of the shareholder barons who will sell the enterprise or their shares any day is the innocence of a masochist. Working for the sustainability of the enterprise is what knowledge workers can devote their knowledge to and actualize their potentials to go beyond their own expectations.

2

The LCD Syndrome

'... The fabrication of economic man drives a wedge of distrust into society, between our individual wants and our social needs. When everyone merely calculates, we end up with a scheming society... If capitalism stands only for individualism, it will collapse too. For we live as individuals in a social space: We certainly need individual initiative but embedded in social engagement.'

MINTZBERG[5] ET AL. (2002)

Organizations wail about lack of leadership initiative. Intellectuals and academics go hoarse about lack of values in decision or policy making. Attrition in organizations runs at a high. Financial markets the world over move mountains of wealth towards the wealthy while those in penury see hope of salvation dwindling with each day that passes by. Corruption at the highest echelons of industry and governments keep ascending, while corruption of minds across the social hierarchy runs endemic. Even the educated middle class with better paying jobs and lifestyles hanker for more and more while being ready to make compromises on values or ethics. Each to his

---

[5] Mintzberg, H., Simons, R, Basu, K., (2002), 'Beyond Selfishness', MIT Sloan Management Review, Fall 2002, Vol. 44, Issue 1

own, narrowly focussed on the shortest term is the common denominator most settle with. Leadership for the long-term, greatness, ethics, and social responsibility are luxuries to be shunned as untenable or impossible. It is the lowest common denominator (LCD) Syndrome that reigns supreme in organizations and the society at large.

James Freeman Clarke (1810–1888), an American theologian and author said, 'A politician thinks of the next election. A statesman, of the next generation'. We see the same even today. It is this LCD Syndrome that gave rise to the hoard-it-all politicians in most democracies and obliterated the genes of the statesman. It is the same malaise that probably rang the death knell for the virtues of socialism. It is what created the king of averages, the Ellsworth Tooheys[6] or the all-powerful media as the king makers, whose need for TRPs makes them glamorize even the most questionable characters in politics as leaders. It is the same condition that prevents statesmen or leaders to pass the LCD test in today's world.

How Did We Degenerate to This Level of LCD?

On the societal plane, the industrial revolution leading to economic surplus for some led the others to somehow think, decide, and act on whatever that could lead them to economic surplus. After all, economic surplus is the easiest way to fulfil the basic needs of man—survival needs followed by self-esteem. Loftier needs like love, respect, intellectual satisfaction, and self-actualization can be postponed for gratification as concluded by Maslow himself. Economic surplus makes an individual stand tall in his immediate society—I am comparatively better off. And more and more succeeded, following the 'survival of the

---

[6] Rand, A., (1946), *The Fountainhead*, The Caxton Printers, Ltd.

fittest and luckiest' logic. Consumerism drives buyers and gladly catered to by the seller. Time comes to a standstill, anti-aging therapy sells at a premium, and personal PATs zoom without proportional increase in the national per capita income. Why blame the simplistic American, everyone across the world appears to have become an expert in nose-tip management. Goals like greatness, ethics, innovation, or the next generation belong to elitist workshops. Today is what one lives for, tomorrow is assured by the stock investments and mortgages. Fatalism creeps in to the realms of pragmatism. Why worry about leaders in true spirit or statesmen—they belong to the bygones!

Most educated people find it futile to support the righteous politician and accept the best compromise offering immediate solutions. Television channels selling pipedreams of soap operas make more money than those featuring serious debates on education policies. Company boards tend to draw succour from organization structures that do not need leaders with volitional traits but are fine with 'motivated' managers working on programmed logic as per performance management systems (PMS) embedded in matrix structures. There are no material problems, barring the need to acquire more materials. Why do we need to plan or strategize for tomorrow, our today is busy enough—this could last forever! That is the pronounced outlook of the more fortunate in both urban or rural India who have tasted some rewards of the economic development over the last decade or two.

> *We are wallowing in surplus. Why think of those rusty deficit management philosophies like 'cut your coat according to your cloth'?*

The educated society is about the urban class, the relative fortunates. We are where opportunities have multiplied and have dumped us in the surplus with the potential to fulfil merely the *lower needs* of the compulsively comparative man. We are inhaling this intoxicating aroma as in a *shisha* bar, unmindful of what is beyond the haze of our today's achievements.

On the organizational plane, matrix organizations have rightfully taken over, necessary to manage a surfeit of information, skills, diversity, tasks, projects, orders, etc. Knowledge sharing has become more important than knowledge creation, costs more significant than growth, individuals are appreciated for turning into clones, and efficiency is the call of the day, not remarkable achievements. Stretch targets, matrices, and PMS are trusted to take care of nose-tip objectives. Great management programmes are unleashed to trace 'who moved my cheese' instead of developing new varieties of low fat cheese. Strategies are outsourced from consulting companies as the LCD in the organizations near nadirs. Meet our expectations and you will be rewarded. Execution becomes a manager's life while leadership becomes behavourial training instead of leading for growth or development. Why develop people when they need to be only dots in a matrix? People are inefficient and ask too many questions, dots don't—they only perform as per the next quarter's metrics.

> *Surplus was never natural to the homo sapiens; deficit was what it was programmed for.*

Come surplus, the Tooheys became kingmakers, numbers and faceless shareholders became kings, and the celebrated knowledge worker, the prized Pomeranian on a designer leash. Mr Drucker would have shed a bucket of tears bemoaning the fate of his beloved knowledge worker. Just like the royal court jesters or musicians of yore, creativity or innovation thrives in the courts of the Googles, Facebooks, or digital game companies catering largely to those wallowing in comparative surpluses. Gay are the lives of the innocent who frequent the bars and pubs sprouting around their BPO cafeteria-cum-offices as were the coal miners in the then Europe drinking their livers off after a hard days toil. Live for today evening, tomorrow is another party!

And then we hear the lament about lack of innovation, lack of decision making, problem solving, erosion of values, need for anti-corruption codes, corporate social responsibility going amiss, while all investments in the stock markets suddenly vaporize. Mortgages on the third house do not get paid, bankers have to ask builders to reduce prices so that they can get some portion of their NPAs back. So many problems crop up with the surplus brigade, while those in deficit remain in larger deficit. Divorce, disintegrating families, suicides, desolation and old age diseases match numbers with ever increasing shopping malls, downtowns, expensive restaurants, and cars.

Naked capitalism controlled by the short-term greed of the stock markets has created more relative poverty than social harmony or individual happiness. Spiritual gurus are in high demand with the well-heeled as their major clientele. Inflation and endless deficit financing is the norm for artificial opulence. The LCD Syndrome is fed by the daily game of meeting very low level expectations and creating short-term surpluses. Most are scared to think of the long-term and hence interested in the next election not generation, measuring quarterly EBITs not market shares, asking others to meet targets not create their own visions for growth or development.

Is There a Way Out of This LCD Syndrome?

Let us start by being proud of being human beings and then ask ourselves to live its potential in every context. We are also animals and animals are driven only by survival needs or the short-term. But, we are blessed with minds to think beyond the short-term. What is it that will make us think of the long-term other than our own vision about our very own lives?

Let us try to make a few choices between the following options:

1. Do we wish to die with a smile on our lips reminiscing about what we left behind in the *minds* of others? Or die with pride bordering on arrogance, thinking about the financial assets we left behind?
2. Do we wish to acquire all that we want with the most deficit financing available today and forfeit 20+ years of future earnings for enjoying today to the hilt? Or, focus on what little we can enjoy with our present incomes and rather save for the unforeseen future?
3. Do we really *need* to be better off than our neighbour in every material aspect? Or do we wish to invest our spare time and cash into what we really like to do as our very own passionate engagement?
4. Is everything we desire, our need? Or, we do have a few needs that we need to fulfil today, some wants to be worked out after five years and a few dreams that we would like to live longer for?
5. Do we wish to be admired for what we possess and view them as status symbols? Or, do we wish to be respected for our wisdom and be happy?

6. Do we wish our children to crave every kind of junk food and possess every new gadget on the market? Or, do we want them to be healthy, self-motivated individuals respected in their adulthood?
7. Do we wish to have all the best ideas ourselves? Or, do we want to see our juniors come up with them and implement them?
8. Do we wish to be the only happy person we know? Or, we want to have many happy people around us?
9. Should our self-esteem solely come from what material comforts we enjoy? Or, is it possible it comes from what we do and what we have learnt?
10. Do we wish to repent upon where, when, of whom, or as what we were born? Or, are we strong enough to develop ourselves from where we are?

I have no doubts that you will have similar answers to what I can come up with. I also believe that it is not so easy to live by these choices. But, relying on our minds to make a choice on the above questions does act as a powerful antigen to fight the LCD virus we are subjected to every waking moment of our lives.

It appears to me that the human life is the most severe clinical trial for a creation, rife with all kinds of temptations, risks, and challenges. To fail is what it is ordained for. To celebrate a human life is the test of leadership.

Let us try in every daily aspect of our life to harness our human power of living beyond expectations—beyond the short-term. We are on the brink of a Cultural Revolution and it can be led by knowledge worker managers leading the way. You cannot lose, as your knowledge is your insurance.

3

Making a Point

'All Power is within you; you can do anything and everything.'

SWAMI VIVEKANANDA

Do we live just to make a point? Just to make a point to every person, every group of people, and every collective that we have to relate to or transact with?

What is the point?

By the time we pause and reflect on whether or not there is a point, we may have spent more than half of our lives. Till that moment dawns upon us, we have been 'making a point' almost every living day since our birth. We cried and wailed to our parents when our biological demands were merely delayed. Later, we yelled and quarrelled to make a point and used the ultimate weapon of emotional blackmail on our parents or friends/family who loved and cared for us. We made our point at school, among acquaintances we met. Adolescence made us make our point tirelessly until we succeeded to carve out our space as an individual. It is like a game of fencing that we keep playing every waking moment. Some moments of peace and careless reflection did come by but only after we achieved a...*touché!*

Thereafter, we start fencing with stronger and sharper swords in the adult arena; at work, at home, and in the society. We are constantly fighting to ward off someone else encroaching on our space, turf, rights, values, responsibilities, and on our point of view.

Okay! We've made our point. We got our space, our turf, and our freedom finally. It was as if we spent all our life to secure ourselves from some predator. Why do we feel so insecure, so threatened, and finally so lonely and abandoned?

Is it because we somehow believed we live in a jungle, where every other creature is trying to overpower us or annihilate us? Or is it because we are scared of being a face in the crowd, insignificant, meaningless, and obscure! I believe it is more of the latter. I believe it is the relatively unfulfilled inner need for acknowledgement, love, affection, or respect that prevents us from celebrating our own identity.

It is that pinch of narcissism that makes us feel surrounded by predators and at the end behave like predators to others. Obviously, when we all behave as predators, the society that we live in becomes one of predators—a vicious cycle where one preys on the other as he is apprehensive of being preyed upon.

Alas! A beautiful life and its human potential get wasted in our quest for self-esteem. We end up being a mere prisoner in our self-created jungle. If only, we were lucky to have had a more connected parenting. If only we were made to feel more secure, more wanted, more cared for and loved, we could have lived a life beyond such short-term expectations of ourselves.

The *Touché* individual—one who is always looking to make a point—finds his natural habitat in organizations where the environment is largely influenced by the archaic 'command and control' management culture. Douglas McGregor warned against this command and control culture more than half a century ago in his seminal book, *The Human Side of Enterprise*[7]. He diagnosed the root cause of this culture to be the economic basis, that 'employees' are dependent on their 'employers' (represented by their managers) for the fulfilment of their basic needs. The power of managers to support or threaten such need fulfilment is what gave them the belief to practice Theory X (Fig. 3). McGregor went on to propose the Theory Y aimed at organizational integration—'the creation of conditions such that the members of an organization can achieve their own goals best by aligning their efforts towards the success of the enterprise'. The contrast between Theory X and Y is shown in the figure below:

Theory X rests on three core assumptions

- The average human being has an inherent dislike of work and will avoid it if he can.
- Because of this human characteristic of dislike of work, most people must be coerced, controlled, directed, threatened with punishment to get them to put adequate effort toward the achievement of organisational objectives.
- The average human being prefers to be directed, wishes to avoid responsibility, has relatively little ambition, wants security above all.

The human side - 'mediocrity of the masses' - of the economic enterprise today is fashioned from the above propositions and beliefs.

Theory X offers management an easy rationalization for ineffective performance. It is due to the nature of the human resources with which we must work.

Theory Y is based on the following assumptions

- The expenditure of physical & mental efforts in work is as natural as play or rest...
- Man will exercise self-direction and self-control in the service of objectives to which he is committed.
- Commitment to objectives is a function of the rewards associated with their achievements...
- The average human being learns, under proper conditions, not only to accept but to seek responsibility...
- The capacity to exercise a relatively high degree of imagination, ingenuity and creativity in solving organisational problems is widely distributed in the population.
- In modern industrial life, the intellectual potential of the average human being are partly utilized.

Theory Y places the problems squarely in the lap of management (managers).

FIG. 3 – THEORY X VS THEORY Y

---

[7] Recommend reading the annotated edition of *The Human side of Enterprise* by Douglas McGregor, Tata McGraw-Hill, 2006

Theory X essentially ignores human depth and potential and creates a predatory environment in organizations. People working in such environments of distrust are forced to behave as predators or subjugate. Most try to safeguard their interests for fulfilment of their basic needs as they are made to feel so dependent or threatened for their security and self-esteem. Sadly, unfulfilled self-esteem needs appear to be the root cause for managers to practice as Theory X types.

The second reason that Theory X still rules the roost in most organizations and influences the working behaviour of most managers is the hugely misplaced obsession with the short-term economic performance of an enterprise. We all know that economic performance is not about the next quarter. It is about sustainability in the long-term. Mere economic principles may *calculate* economic results in the long-term, but help to *achieve* only short-term results. It is the human side of the enterprise that ensures the long-term growth of an enterprise. And that is not possible by just making a point! The Touché individuals need to grow up into organizational adults or mature into managers to develop long-term mindsets if the basic economic objective of an enterprise—sustained profitable growth—has to be successfully fulfilled. By default, if not design, this may even develop managers into conscientious leaders.

Till now we played with the manager–leader divide and the contexts the manager has to manage or work in. The next part on Managerial Science is designed to equip the manager with both the armour and the armoury.

PART 3

The Science for Managers

This part strings together the main beads of the Practising Manager's Growth Mantra

- *'Managers: Professionals under Pressure' deals with the Manager's ardent need for professional knowledge and its challenges. This section pirouettes around the professional, the Manager, and presents the Manager's Achilles' Heel. It helps Managers relate to the unique role and potential that they ALONE have and can enjoy.*
- *'Motivation Arena' shows the blatant use of Abraham Maslow's Theory of Motivation in the managerial world. Sadly, they address only the lower half of the need hierarchy. This section raises a serious question about the application of motivation theory in leadership development, if not sealing its fate.*
- *'The Volition Arena' takes you to the world of 'free will'. Volitional psychology has been sparingly discussed by academics in the domain of management and is yet to be used as a fundamental in management. As a practitioner, I have found volitional engagement to be the most powerful ingredient in a manager's evolution into a leader. Most, if not all, 'remarkable achievements' are based upon volitional engagements. Motivation theory hardly pays for the passage!*
- *'The Narcissist' sheds light on why leadership positions attract narcissists like bees to honey. Most management practitioners could do well to be aware of the risks and take home a few hints for managing this pathological tendency that most of us carry with us.*

1

Managers: Professionals Under Pressure

'...the professional draws upon the knowledge of science and of his colleagues and upon knowledge gained through his own experience. The degree to which he relies upon the first two of these rather than the third is one of the ways in which the professional (manager) may be distinguished from a layman'.

PROF. DOUGLAS MCGREGOR

Before we go into the science of knowledge that a manager needs to draw upon to not be just a layman as cautioned by McGregor, let us look at what a manager goes through to realize the lack of that professional knowledge. This is important as the first milestone of any learning cycle for all of us is being 'consciously incompetent'. In any context in life, something happens to make us realize that we are not adequately equipped to handle what falls on our plate. This realization motivates us to reach the next milestone of 'conscious competence' when we make a choice to learn the missing competence and grasp it enough to start using it. As we go on practising the competence gained consciously, we gradually mature into the final but continuous stage of 'unconscious competence' till we are hit again by changed contexts to embark on another journey up the learning curve.

A manager is just like any other civilized human being. His life is full of responsibilities, results, knowledge usage and creation, conflicting goals, opposition, values, needs, and aspirations. He is educated, has opinions and normally has a family to take care of. It is the same family where he retires into each night to return hopefully with renewed vigour and energy for another day at work.

Work is where he deals with deadlines, results, and people with differing views, likes, dislikes, and conflicts of all kinds. All that, while he keeps performing as a manager, not get rattled with office politics, accept some irrational decisions around, and get a normal pay raise.

Managers are professionals under pressure.

You are under pressure to perform and delegate; pressure to perform as a parent, as a spouse, and at times as an 'adult child' or even as a guardian to your ageing parents. You are under pressure to create more wealth and fast and consistently under pressure to manage a work–life balance.

Like many managers, I too had to go through all that. I struggled to find my work–life balance only to realize that work is a subset of life and hence it cannot be a war between life (the superset) and work (Fig. 4).

What needs to balance work is not the entire life on the other side, but additional things that we would love to do, other than the work we *have* to do as a part of our karma. On the organizational front, in the earlier phase of my life as a manager, I was doing a lot of great things myself and growing. With growth came more responsibilities as well as the opening

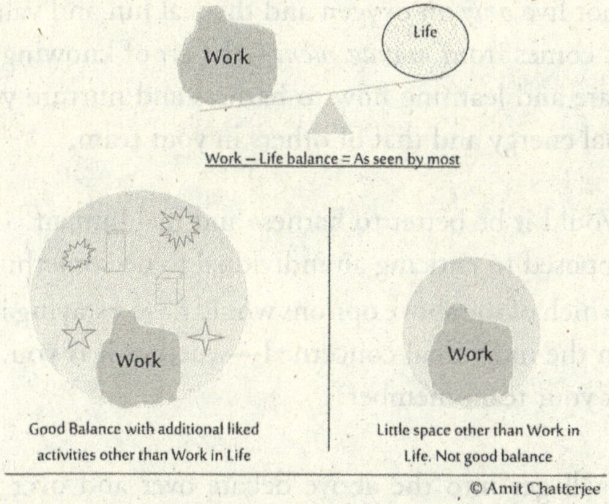

FIG. 4 – THE NEW WORK–LIFE BALANCE

of more frontiers than what I as an individual could attempt to breach. I was a sales manager then and the sheer number of customers the business could grow into became a statistical impossibility for me alone to handle. I realized that I was the bottleneck to capturing the potential of growth and the only way to keep the organization growing was to develop others and make myself relatively redundant. This realization itself was enough to relieve the pressure on me. Although, the quantity of work or time I had to devote to develop others did not change my work–life balance, the quality of the task realized and chosen by me gave me more energy than it took away. Developing others was something I loved to do. In hindsight, I can say, while it is true that managers are professionals under pressure, the pressure really gets diffused when we choose to do something and enjoy doing it.

In time, I came to understand that while skills and domain knowledge were too important, they were like oxygen without which it is not possible for any team or individual to work. But, we do not live *only* on oxygen and the real fun and value of life or work comes from *management*—the art of knowing yourself as you are and learning how to harness and nurture your own volitional energy and that of others in your team.

1. Would it be better to harness and fuel human volition as opposed to enticing an individual to do something?
2. Which of the above options would have a staying influence on the individual concerned—whether it is you, yourself or your team member?

We will get into the above debate over and over again in this book. I leave you to make your choice in the meanwhile. Remember, the first unique thing that a leader does is making a choice as opposed to just trying to do his best with what falls in his lap.

Unique Challenge and Potential of Being a Manager

As I went through the experiences in my role as a manager, every tussle or ruffle I had to handle made me see my relative incompetence for the contexts I had to manage. I had reached the 'conscious incompetence' stage of my managerial learning cycle.

In our professional journey, a stage comes when we have climbed the better part of the initial learning curve and suddenly, we get ushered into the role of a manager. The elation of hauling ourselves up one last incline after climbing up a steep hill for some time is almost like being embraced by the hugging warmth of a much awaited sunrise.

As we merrily slip into the manager's chair, we hardly realize that this seat has its own trajectory and potential. We do know that this ushers us into the world of management responsibilities. It is what we aspired for and even hankered after the accoutrements of being a manager without realizing what the position holds in store. It is like *Abhimanyu* getting into the *Chakravyu*[8] without any idea about how to survive there. Only a manager faces the unique challenge to be 'good' in a domain for which he is neither trained nor experienced enough!

Let us consider a scenario. An experienced design engineer was working as a Team Leader for one of the four teams in the R&D department of a fast growing company. He was promoted by his management as the R&D Manager when his manager decided to move on. He was known for being a task master and his team's performance on project deliverables had gone up markedly over the past three years under him. He was very knowledgeable in his domain and a stickler for discipline. He always took complete ownership for all the projects that his team had to work on and rarely failed on deadlines or commitments. A darling of his management, he won the promotion hands down when the opportunity opened up. After the congratulations and dinners ended, he dived into his role as the big manager with his characteristic intensity. Over the next year and a half, he worked like a man possessed to bring up the efficiency and discipline for the other teams now under his charge. He was doing his best to fulfil the expectations of his management.

Some rumblings and grumblings became part of the grapevine in the meanwhile. At the end of the second year,

---

[8] From *Mahabharata*, the Indian epic. *Chakravyu* could be related to 'Complexity'. *Abhimanyu*, the capable fighter son of the great archer *Arjuna*, had learnt from his illustrious father how to get into the *Chakravyu* but did not know how to manage it. Yet, he chose to enter it!

his management recognized the need for intervention when HR reported a spurt in attrition among the junior engineers and one of the team leaders had just put in his papers. But, by this time our new manager was already quite a frazzled man. He could not understand what went wrong. He had worked with all sincerity and never had any agenda to hurt anyone. He only expected from all his team leaders what he would ask of himself—discipline, meeting commitments, and efficiency. His people complained of workload, late hours, feared him, and had started to even avoid him. Some had even labelled him a slave driver.

The management put him on a mentorship programme and that helped him a lot. He realized the value of empathy and fun while working with a diverse team and managing four team leaders. He realized that he as an individual never said 'No' to his management and always ended up with more on his plate than what his department could chew. He also realized that his colleagues and team members had needs and interests beyond the working skills and domain knowledge. The team leader, who resigned after two years with him, said in his exit interview how he looked up to him during their peer days and believed that he was the right choice for the R&D Manager position when it fell vacant. But after some months of working with his former peer, now his manager, he started to have problems in his family life. It went from bad to worse due to his having to frequently take work back home or work late. He said that he was never able to share anything with his manager about his personal challenges other than technical- or project-related topics.

Only a manager faces the unique challenge to be 'good' in a role for which he is neither trained nor experienced enough. In not too much time, the initial romance of the loving embrace of the sun wanes and we start feeling the chill at the hilltop.

We kick off our new job as a manager and also intern for the same role at the same time. In hindsight, one would call it managerial experience that was never enough! We start gaining the competence and wisdom in miniscule doses while getting scorched by the noontime sun without much respite. We look forward to the nights when we would hide under the darkness of solitude, catch some slumber only to raise ourselves to another day of surprises, newness, conflicts, decisions, and guilt. We seek guidance from our seniors only to see them smirk at our bewilderment. We feel relieved to meet a few who offer some words of advice or pass on a fat book written by some haloed academic. We want to read these books and do start them only to be jerked awake by another managerial tussle.

This part and the rest of the book brings into focus the gaps in managerial knowledge and the development potential emanating from it. By the time we become managers, we never question ourselves about our professional knowledge in the domain we work in. We are at our prime and the thought never crosses our mind that we of all people may lack the professional knowledge to effectively play the role of a Manager. Most managers are fluent about the results their organization has to produce and the skills, processes, the technology, deadlines, and resources they need to deliver the results. They say quite readily and surely, 'Rest assured, I will do my best'. They do try their best, but…

Some years back, I had to take over a business unit that needed a deep overhaul in almost all functions. While running the transformation in our operations, my head of operations, the GM in the Fig. 5 was on board with me and the rest of my management team. He was a fine gentleman on whom I could depend for integrity and commitment. One evening, as we sat down to discuss the hurdles he was facing with his managers in implementing changes we had agreed upon the topic narrowed upon the individuals he had to deal with and how they were responding to the changes. As it turns out, such management discussions about real human beings or managers take much more time than normal meetings on inanimate matters like processes, budgets, or technology. Now, my GM was a good engineer with twenty years behind him, having started in technical sales and then moving on to operations. Like most managers, he too had risen from the trenches and was adroit in supporting his team in all technical or business issues. But, in change management one deals a lot with matters of the 'animate(d)', where you are unravelling issues related to the heart or minds of people.

To explain a way out for how he could better handle some of the implementation hurdles he was facing with two of his managers, I referred to the merits of McGregor's Theory Y instead of Theory X. With all the pressures we were going through at that time, a discussion on McGregor and his theories was a bit taxing for my good friend. But, I believed that it would do him and us a lot of good once he understood McGregor's explanation about the strengths of Theory Y and could make use of it.

Sensing his impatience with such topics, I stopped my explanation on theories and asked him, 'What are you?' He replied tersely, 'I am an engineer.' And that he was a good one too. I stepped in further to ask about his production manager who reported to him and the bright young production engineer he liked a lot. He replied intently, 'They too are engineers.' He was probably already getting to where I was headed. All three of them were mechanical engineers. I asked him, 'Who among you three deals with mechanical engineering the most and who the least?' His answer was immediate. The production engineer was handling mechanical engineering issues the most and he, the big boss of operations, the least. Then I asked him my big question, 'Why does the company then pay you the most?' My colleague was really good. His straight face broke into a sheepish smile, and he said, 'Well, I am a manager and not just an engineer.' My last question to my GM was, 'Look, you all studied mechanical engineering for becoming good engineers and of course you have the most experience in the application of engineering knowledge but, just think of what you studied to be a good manager?' He accepted, although a bit hesitatingly, that he and his managers could invest formally in management learning. The graphic in Fig. 5 was what I drew on my desk calendar that day. I named it as the Achilles' Heel of all managers.

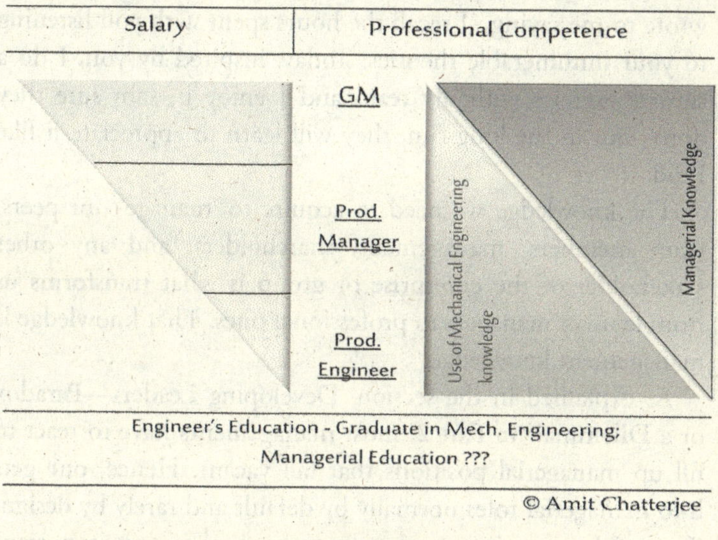

FIG. 5 – THE MANAGER'S ACHILLES' HEEL

I have no qualms in admitting that I was NOT referring to MBA education at all when I spoke about management education. My colleague accepted the argument but also realized that it is not so easy to get 'management education' overnight. Most of us become managers without appropriate education or training for our managerial or leadership roles. I had to and did complete the topic of McGregor's Theory X & Y with my GM another day, when he was a bit more relaxed from the daily grind of change management. Later, we went on to sponsor our managers and potential managers for management education where application of theory to practice is the pivot. I must admit that not many exist but a lot of business schools have realized it and are gradually evolving their curriculum to address this urgent need for management education. The GM went on to grow in another organization as a VP and recently wrote to me saying, 'I recall the hours spent with you listening to your innumerable theories. Today, inspired by you, I do a similar exercise with my team and I enjoy it, (am sure they don't) but in the long run, they will learn to appreciate it like I did.'

The knowledge we need to acquire to 'manage' our peers, team members, management, shareholders, and any other stakeholder of the enterprise or group is what transforms us from layman managers to professional ones. That knowledge is management knowledge.

As explained in the section 'Developing Leaders—Paradox or a Dilemma?' in Part 2, most managements have to react to fill up managerial positions that fall vacant. Hence, one gets into managerial roles normally by default and rarely by design. Succession planning is already recognized as an important requirement practiced in most modern organizations today, but yet largely remains in the reported database of the HR function instead of becoming an important part of a manager's conscious repertoire and agenda. The reason for this apparent knowledge amnesia could be due to an obsession with short-term results and a wishful imagery of the manager being more perennial than the enterprise. Well, if managers are not thinking of growing enterprises beyond their professional lifetimes, succession planning could remain an agenda point of the HR but never see the light of the day in succession development as development of successors or the next generation of leaders can only be done by their functional managers. Development of the next generation of managers and learning how to manage different animate stakeholders would need us to look into the role of a manager anew.

One needs to look into this management knowledge as a huge complement to the inanimate aspects like processes, tools, systems, skills, technology, etc. This management knowledge of managing the animate side of an enterprise's growth is what demands leadership and brings out the professional in a manager. This does motivate a manager to realize the unique challenge and potential of being a manager in an organization.

Manager's Role and Knowledge Gaps

Reams have been published on the manager's role. The textbooks say management is to plan, organize, coordinate, and control. It does sound right, but down in the trenches, the manager's job turns out to be far more complicated. In fact, you play so many roles, it is hard to excel at any one. I take for this occasion the definition or prescriptions offered by two of the top legendary management gurus.

Peter Drucker said the Manager's role is about five tasks:

1. Set objectives—The manager sets goals for the group, and decides what work needs to be done to meet those goals.
2. Organizes—The manager divides the work into manageable activities, and selects people to accomplish the tasks that need to be done.
3. Motivates and communicates—The manager creates and integrates a team out of his people through decisions on pay, placement, promotion, and through his communications with the team.
4. Measures—The manager establishes appropriate targets and yardsticks and analyses, appraises, and interprets performance.
5. Develops people—With the rise of the knowledge worker, this task has taken on added importance. In a knowledge economy, people are the company's most important asset and it is up to the manager to develop that asset.

I take the underlined words to form 'The Manager's Maxim'. Herein resides the hidden 'principles of managerial science' for the knowledge society we live in today:

> *'The Manager sets goals, decides, and selects PEOPLE to accomplish the tasks. He motivates and communicates to integrate people, while being responsible for their development.'*

The non-underlined parts are more about what I call the 'inanimate' topics like the work process, the knowledge and skills for the work to be done, the planning that goes into the quantitative aspects, and finally the value of work to determine appropriate compensation. Now, these are basics of the 'craft and economics' of management, akin to oxygen and water that we need for mere survival. The craft and economics of work was laid out more than adequately a century ago by Frederick Taylor with his path breaking Time–Work studies in 1911. These principles were good enough to propel companies like Ford ahead of competition who could afford then to be dependent on craft–and art-based automobile production.

The Manager's Maxim relevant today is instead about the 'animate(d)' aspects of the work environment. The application of the Manager's Maxim would make us realize that it is all about the people who have to be convinced about the goals as much as the manager. It is about the *drivers* that make the manager take decisions. It is about learning how to select the right personalities and mindsets for the context in hand. It is about how the manager communicates the decisions, goals, and roles to his people. It is about how a subordinate looks up to her manager and senses the sincerity about her own development. All the above is locked into this maxim that 'motivates' people. Appropriate work compensation packages—however refined and clever they may be—based upon correct yet age old concepts from Adam Smith[9] are not enough to engage people in the knowledge society.

There is no avoiding the fact that most of us who become managers or get into management positions are not really prepared to handle this role. We never had to do it till we became managers, although, we could have been lucky to have experienced or observed such *management* in our personal lives in our (or as) parents or grandparents.

---

[9] Smith, Adam, (1776–89), *An Inquiry into the Nature and Causes of the Wealth of Nations*, London: Methuen and Co., Ltd., ed. Edwin Cannan, 1904. Fifth edition

Henry Mintzberg[10] observes that the pressures of a manager's job can drive one to:

- ➢ Take on too much work
- ➢ Operate with constant interruptions
- ➢ Respond prematurely to complex events
- ➢ Act rather than think
- ➢ Make decisions without seeing the big picture

The above statements are nothing but red flags from the guru. It only chastens us to prepare better before we embark on our journey as managers. Mintzberg identifies 10 different roles under three categories of managerial dispensation. This sounds even more complex than Drucker's prescription:

Interpersonal roles

1. Figurehead—You represent your group to your organization and the community at large.
2. Leader—You hire, train, and motivate employees.
3. Liaison—You maintain contact with colleagues and stakeholders outside your immediate chain of command.

Informational Roles

4. Monitor—You leverage your personal network to scan the environment for vital information.
5. Disseminator—You feed information to subordinates who lack your access to critical data.
6. Spokesperson—You provide information on behalf of your unit to senior management and outside organizations.

---

[10] Mintzberg, H., (1990), *Harvard Business Review* March–April 1990.

Decisional Roles

7. Entrepreneur—You initiate projects to improve your unit's processes or profits.
8. Disturbance Handler—You manage crises caused by precipitated by employees, customers, suppliers, systems, or accidents.
9. Resource Allocator—You decide who will get what, coordinate the impact of interrelated decisions, and allocate managerial time.
10. Negotiator—You use strategic information to resolve grievances, establish contracts, and promote shared decisions.

What is additional in Mintzberg's prescription than Drucker's is the role of a leader (one could collate the different asks in line with the context to be managed). What is common is decision making and the dominant focus on an intelligent need for communication, whether to your own people, your peers, bosses, or other stakeholders.

None of the above prescriptions (choose Drucker, Mintzberg, or anyone from the plethora of other management academics, who are more correct than wrong in their studies on organizations) are about skills that people learn in their non-managerial job in a formal manner. The knowledge to practice the manager's role is not gained from having been good at engineering, finance, marketing, HR, legal, production or quality functions. All functions in an organization need managers and the science or knowledge needed to excel in their roles comes from domains that they have normally not studied or practiced. The textbooks say that the Manager's role is to *predict and control the results* of their domains and dwell primarily on the 'inanimate' aspects of the managerial role—again correctly!

This led to the belief in and practice of McGregor's Theory X by default, where managers interpreted the textbooks' asks as *predict, command and control human behaviour instead of the results.* And they tried to control behaviour largely banking on the use of Maslow's theory by negotiating expectations of the employer vis-à-vis that of the employee. There was a time when the manager or a foreman in an industrial era factory didn't have to give much thought to the people who were producing. His job was to organize the work, assign the right people to the necessary tasks, give instructions, coordinate the results, and ensure the job got done as ordered. The focus was on efficiency and controlling the work ethics of the people through his power over what drove their need fulfilment.

In the knowledge economy, however—where value is increasingly a function of the knowledge worker and they are no longer undifferentiated cogs in an industrial machine—people look to their managers, not just to be assigned a task, but to define for them a purpose. The manager's role is the only role in an organization today which plays with uncertainty and opposition, giving rise to conflicts of thought as well as among individuals. As most managers get trained on the job for their managerial roles, they are bound to make more errors than those in other roles in an organization.

Hence, it could be very useful to invest your time in the science as well as art of management. The science comes from the known concepts, theories, principles of management, whereas the art enters at a slower pace through practising management, learning through observation, and your own reflections.

While 'The Human Side of Enterprise' from Douglas McGregor remains an emancipating read for most knowledge workers or managers even after 56 years of his landmark speech at the MIT, the three other topics I have found most useful in my practice as a manager are Maslow's Theory of Human Motivation[11], Volitional Psychology, and Narcissism. In the following pages, I have tried to give a practitioner's take on these topics, discussing more on the application rather than just the theory. I believe that these theories, concepts, and the experience of using them as science in management forms the principal basis of professional knowledge for a manager. In the later chapters, we go back to the practitioner's mind and life again and see how the science of management plays out in harnessing and fuelling managerial or leadership practice.

[11] Maslow, A., (1943), 'A Theory of Human Motivation' Psychological Review #50(1943) p. 370–396

2

The Motivation Arena

'It is not from the benevolence of the butcher, the brewer, or the baker, that we expect our dinner; but from their regard to their own interest. We address not to their humanity but to their self-love.'

ADAM SMITH (1776)

We hear and use the word motivation in the organizational world more often than anything else. Even the term leadership does not escape from being constantly shadowed by this word and get blurred enough to make most believe as if they were the same thing. We normally hear of it when a manager is expected to motivate people working for her to be able to perform as planned or desired. This does amount to 'controlling' the behaviour of others to deliver the results that the manager is accountable for due to her position of responsibility. Hence, a manager would be better placed to take a pause and be consciously clear about what goes into motivating others. If a manager is interested in leadership, this would also help in understanding what motivates the manager herself.

I looked up the web to see what the word motivation throws up and came up with the following (shorter to longer phrases):

- Providing with a reason to act in a certain way
- Motivation is the purpose or psychological cause of an action
- Motivation is literally the desire to do things. It's the crucial element in setting and attaining goals
- Motivation may be rooted in a basic impulse to optimize well-being, minimize physical pain, and maximize pleasure
- Motivation results from the interaction of both conscious and unconscious factors such as the (1) intensity of desire or need, (2) incentive or reward value of the goal, and (3) expectations of the individual and of his or her peers. These factors are the reasons one has for behaving a certain way
- Extrinsic motivations are those that arise from outside of the individual and often involve rewards such as trophies, money, social recognition or praise. Intrinsic motivations are those that arise from within the individual, such as doing a complicated crossword puzzle purely for the personal gratification of solving a problem
- What comes to your mind when you think of 'motivating' another person? How does your manager try to motivate you? What are the normal motivators used in the organizational world?

Well, Fig. 6 is a bit of a caricature. What is used in organizations is probably more subtle or civilized. Incentives, pay raise, bonus, stock options, profit sharing, promotion, perks, paid holidays, club memberships, titles, company cars, bigger desks/ office, coffee machine, reserved parking, etc., are examples of extrinsic motivators commonly used by managers

FIG. 6 – MOTIVATION ENGINEERED!

or management and will be there to stay as most humans do get motivated by the hope of fulfilling their unfulfilled needs. It is as natural as the lure for food that trappers unfailingly used for centuries to snare their prize catches.

Abraham Maslow did a yeoman's service through his theory on human motivation to explain the basis for any human being (barring none) to feel motivated. I am yet to come across anybody, including myself, on whom Maslow's theory does not find application. I try to capture the essentials of Maslow's Theory of Human Motivation as given below:

- Maslow discovered the fundamental of human nature in the fact that man is a perpetually wanting animal. Once our unconscious is cognitive of an unfulfilled need, our behaviour—thinking, decisions, and even actions are motivated by this ungratified need.

- Next, he identified a 'hierarchy of needs' as shown on the next page in Fig. 7. This hierarchy identifies the basic needs of man.
- He found these basic goals related to each other, being arranged in a hierarchy of prepotency. This means that the most prepotent (or higher) goal will monopolize consciousness and influence the mind to organize various capacities of the individual.

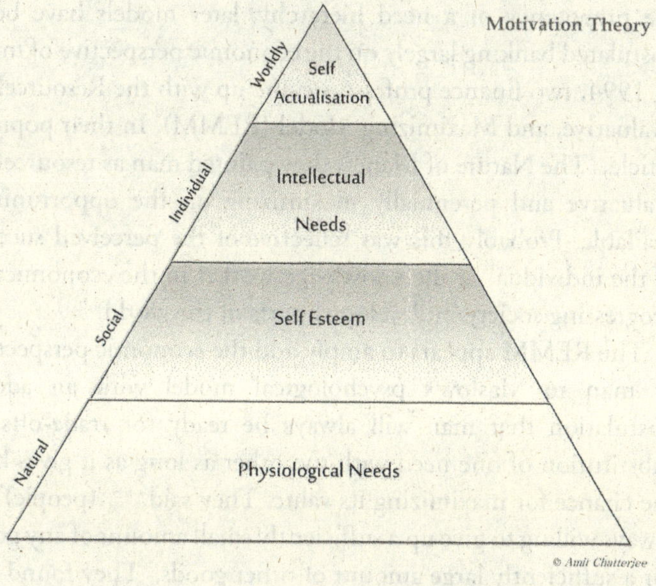

FIG. 7 – MASLOW'S HIERARCHY OF NEEDS

- Maslow observed, 'The less prepotent needs are minimized, even forgotten or denied. But when a need is fairly well satisfied, the higher or the next prepotent need emerges, in turn to dominate the conscious life and to serve as the centre of organization of behaviour, since gratified needs are not active motivators.' (It is like a salary rise in the offing that motivates us to keep doing the good work. But, the moment we have got the raise, it stops motivating us anymore.)

Combined with the obvious need of an enterprise to achieve sustained economic success, evolution of the knowledge society has also led to a proliferation of objects of desire and the space for individual expression and demands. While Maslow's theory provides explanation for human behaviour resting on the prepotency of a need hierarchy, later models have been postulated banking largely on the economic perspective of man. In 1994, two finance professors came up with the Resourceful, Evaluative, and Maximizing Model (REMM). In their popular article, 'The Nature of Man'[12], they painted man as resourceful, evaluative and perennially maximizing on the opportunities available. Probably this was reflective of the perceived success of the individual or the knowledge worker in the economically progressing society in developed parts of the world.

The REMM appears to amply add the economic perspective of man to Maslow's psychological model with an added postulation that man will always be ready for trade-offs or substitution of one need with the other as long as it gives him the chance for maximizing its value. They said, '...(people) are always willing to give up a sufficiently small amount of any good for a sufficiently large amount of other goods.' They found the following story as an alibi to their REMM Model.

George Bernard Shaw, the famous playwright and social thinker, reportedly once said that while on an ocean voyage he met a celebrated actress on deck and asked her whether she

[12] Jensen, M. C.and Meckling, W. H., (1994) 'The Nature of Man', Journal of Applied Finance, V. 7, No. 2, p. 4–19.

would be willing to sleep with him for a million dollars. He claimed she was agreeable. He followed with a counterproposal: 'What about ten dollars?' 'What do you think I am?' she responded indignantly. He replied, 'We've already established that—now we're just haggling over price.' George Bernard Shaw was known for his rancour and wit. The above anecdote may be an invention to prove a point. Whichever way, the point his story makes is that individuals are willing to sacrifice a little of almost anything they may care about, even reputation or morality, for a sufficiently large quantity of other desired things.

Acceptance and application of Maslow's theory and add-on concepts like the REMM in organizations and management has been profound. Unfortunately, managers or management marched on trying to negotiate even future needs or the 'wants and desires' of man. This has led to a naked practice of 'give and take' relationships, where the manager or the employer tends to believe that 'their' work will be done by anyone to whom they can offer a higher degree of gratification. It makes management look so easy—one needs to just find what an employee wishes to achieve and negotiate a transactional relationship based on expectations from either side. Meeting expectations is the philosophy that forms the basis for motivating people in management of organizations. Motivation theory as practised by managers has boiled down to measuring and rewarding economic performance with pecuniary and status benefits in cash or kind as such things are easy to connect with the expectation of maximizing their value in the short-term. Such a management culture dependent upon extrinsic motivators, as explained above, has made people succumb to an existence of perennial pursuit of unfulfilled expectations.

In the enterprise world, the pecuniary benefits on offer include incentives, pay raise, bonus, stock options, profit sharing, promotion, perks, paid holidays, club memberships, titles, bigger desks/office, coffee machine, reserved parking, etc. All the above carry the potential to gratify the two lower needs of the Maslow's hierarchy, namely the Physiological and Self-esteem needs. Self–esteem is a need that has no horizon, when bought through financial means. There is no end to better, richer, and flamboyant lifestyles that you could lead with more and more money. Each step you take towards comparative supremacy, the light at the end of the self-esteem tunnel only moves that much farther away.

Hence, extrinsic motivators in the form of pecuniary and status benefits cannot satisfy the self-esteem needs of a person. Man therefore never discovers the higher needs like intellectual needs or self-actualization as explained by Maslow's theory based upon the prepotency model. Intrinsic motivation belongs to the higher levels of the need hierarchy, namely when man is motivated by unfulfilled intellectual or self-actualization needs. If management of an enterprise is blinded solely by the economic perspective of the organization, they will be able to address only the economic perspective of man that largely addresses the shorter term or lower needs of man's need hierarchy. Perennial pursuit of such lower needs renders a man oblivious of long-term objectives or values like greatness, ethics, innovation, creativity, corporate social responsibility, and development of more and more conscientious leaders. And, these are the values that we expect from leadership or managers.

The proof of the above argument is the malaise the society or organizations are in where we are lamenting the lack of leadership, values, and a continuous development of foundations for creating and sustaining growth. The morass we are wallowing in is a direct consequence of organizations and society motivated based on pecuniary and short-term benefits.

The Organizational Hierarchy of Needs

Maslow's hierarchy of needs with its pre-potency model inspired me to apply it to organizations. I was fortunate to spend most of my professional life helping small enterprises develop and grow into market leaders. I enjoyed very much the experience of catapulting people and businesses to grow from relative scratch positions. In hindsight, when I reflect on these journeys and analyse the trajectories, I realize that organizations too behave like individuals.

Organizations too are non-cognitive of higher needs until their lower needs are gratified. The graphic below depicts the Organizational Hierarchy of Needs compared with Maslow's pyramid applicable to mankind.

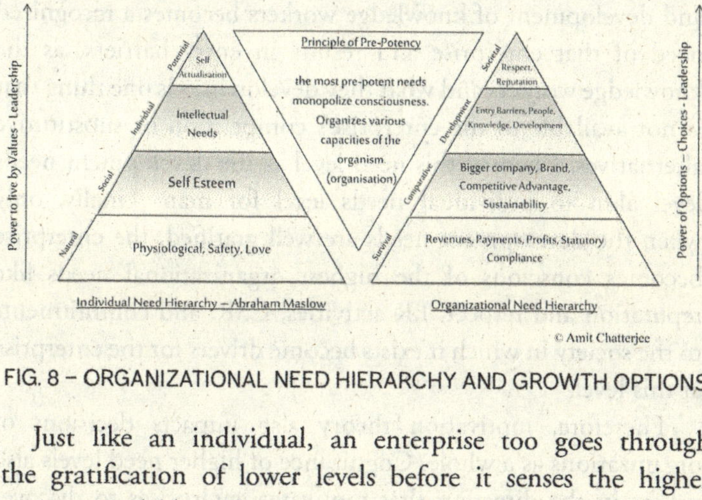

FIG. 8 – ORGANIZATIONAL NEED HIERARCHY AND GROWTH OPTIONS

Just like an individual, an enterprise too goes through the gratification of lower levels before it senses the higher options available and strives for that level. The organizational need hierarchy depicted above shows the lower level needs of revenues, payments, profits, and statutory compliance as the survival state of an enterprise. These can be compared to the physiological needs or the natural level for mankind. Once these basic needs are fulfilled, the enterprise gains cognizance of the next level needs like size, brand, competitiveness, sustainability, nice facades or offices. I refer to this level as comparative need similar to the social needs of an individual. This is when man or an enterprise starts seeing how they are positioned vis-à-vis the outside world and work for comparative supremacy. Once the basic two need levels—survival/natural and comparative/ social —are relatively gratified, the cognizance levels breach the short-term and start investing in sustainability and longer-term objectives.

Just like man, once an enterprise is comfortable with its space in its immediate society (comfortable with its peers on a comparative basis), it identifies consciously with the development potential of its knowledge workers. Retention and development of knowledge workers becomes a recognized need of that enterprise and results in entry barriers, as the knowledge workers and what they develop into is one thing that is not available to the enterprise's competition or substitutive alternatives. I named this need level as the development needs level akin to individual needs level for man. Finally, only when the development needs are well gratified, the enterprise becomes conscious of the highest organizational needs like reputation and respect. PR activities, CSR, and commitments to the society in which it exists become drivers for the enterprise at this level.

Therefore, motivation theory also impacts decisions of organizations as a whole. Cognizance of higher need levels also ushers in the direction that motivates enterprises to discover more options and make new choices. That is when enterprises (management) become conscious about the need for leadership, since development of knowledge or entry barriers or managing a plethora of evolving options is not possible with a handful in management positions. It is just like the value system lived by in case of human beings. As the lower need levels become more and more gratified, man starts sensing the power of values and makes tougher choices as a hygiene factor as shown in the vertical axis in Fig. 8. Working through a value system and making choices are the behavioural signs of a leader, not a task finisher.

Hence, leadership thinking and behaviour surfaces with the gratification of lower needs like physiological and self-esteem needs in case of a human being and survival and comparative needs for an organization. But, obsession with the mere economic perspective of man or an enterprise keeps such entities away from recognizing the higher needs like intellectual or self-actualization needs of man and development and societal needs of an enterprise. This leaves the man stunted in leadership thinking or living by a value system and renders enterprises bereft of innovative options or leadership development. Decisions and actions borne out of mere economic perspective of man or enterprise leads to short-term actions and that is what leads to the morass we are in.

In order to create sustained profitable growth, we need to understand the value of long-term approach in our thinking, decisions, and actions. A differentiation between needs, wants, and dreams may help in managing the natural temptation to be driven by the short-term. It may be worthwhile to ask ourselves the question:

Is everything we desire, our need? Or, do we have a few needs that we need to fulfil today, some wants to be worked out after five years and a few dreams that we would like to live longer for?

Fig. 9 explains how an enterprise can fulfil only 'needs' of all stakeholders in the short-term. Whereas, the 'wants' and 'value to their growth' as value creation is created in the mid and

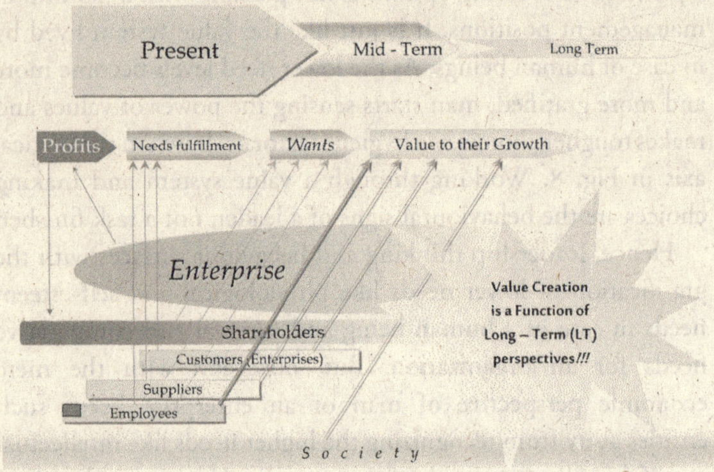

FIG. 9 – VALUE CREATION IS A FUNCTION OF LONG-TERM PERSPECTIVES

long-term. But, freewheeling use of motivational engagement as practiced in most organizations obfuscates the vision of the long-term and keeps people or organizations locked in the world of lower need fulfilment. Hence, we need to look elsewhere to wrench the human mind out of the shackles of motivational imprisonment.

Volitional engagement could be the way out. The next section paves the way into the volitional arena.

3

The Volitional Arena

Three years had gone by since I had taken up the charge as the Sales Manager of the company I run today. I had two gold cards from two top airlines, each with enough miles to reward myself with free vacation travel, anytime I wanted them. The only thing missing was a mental pause to plan vacations. My competitors were not very happy to meet me at airports or customer locations as I was a threat to their success. My team was young in experience and knowledge as the company I worked for was a late entrant in the market. I was looked up to and respected and I wanted my team to grow up into a powerful and successful team (which they did, in due course, in style).

One evening, while I was getting ready to leave for the airport, my wife lobbed an interesting question at me, 'Mr Chatterjee, when are you back in Bangalore…on tour?' The formal address and the '…on tour' bit left a deep cut on my conscience as I bid goodbye to my wife and kids to leave for another sortie out into the market. The driver was struggling to make time through the motocross of Bangalore roads (worse today, after fifteen years), but for a change, our politicians escaped my ire and curses as my mind raced through how to balance my managerial challenges with my family needs.

I was sure that my team members have to grow and take more responsibilities and I wanted them to be as self-driven or volitional as I perceived myself to be. As a small, growing company, we could not just buy the best or most experienced talent, hence motivation came more from a sense of ownership, participation, aspiration, and ambition; in hindsight, from organizational narcissism. Other than dreams, passion, and exemplary behaviour to achieve over-arching goals, there was not much I could offer my team.

Just at that juncture, I chanced upon an article in the *Economic Times* that quoted Prof. Sumantra Ghoshal, then the Professor of Strategy at the London Business School, saying, 'Most of management literature is about the theory of motivation, while if one looks deep it is evident that most remarkable achievements in organizations have been through that of volition.' What I wanted my team to do was definitely remarkable from my point of view. But, I knew nothing more about volition than the simple meaning of the word—free will. Yet, that statement from the Euro Guru spoke volumes to me. It was a eureka moment…and that is when began my quest for 'How to harness and fuel human volition?'

It was 1998 and I started using a laptop for the first time. The above question used to roll incessantly as a screensaver on my laptop. For me, the answer to this question was like an elixir I was searching for which would rid me of all the hurdles I was straddled with. I knew, once I found the answer to how to harness and fuel human volition, my managers would volitionally drive the business and I could spend more time with my family and also find something more challenging for myself. That's it! A simple selfish search for a panacea for all that was not right in my little life.

Over the next few years, I read up all I could lay my hands on—on human behaviour, motivation, and volition theories. I went on to write a small thesis[13] on the same topic later and in the process also got the opportunity to interact with Sumantra Ghoshal and learn from his experiences and findings. My research led me to identify the 'volitional buoys' that could be used to harness and fuel human volition. I revelled in combining my academic pursuit with my managerial challenges. This unique opportunity gave me the chance to shape my concepts as well as evolve a practitioner's way forward towards what I had to practice—growth management. I was not motivated by anyone to do what I did. It was a choice that I made and committed myself to.

Unlike motivation theory, volition theory has not been discussed much in management literature until Sumantra Ghoshal[14] and Heike Bruch found application of the same in their research on organizations in 1990s. My purpose with this section is to familiarize my readers with volition theory and its application in leadership practice. Narziss Ach[15] was probably the first to use experiments to differentiate between motivation and volition. Through his experimental research, Ach showed motivation as something related to desire whereas volition was an engagement of the free will, an expression of the state beyond the threshold where motivation gets converted to

---

[13] Chatterjee A., (2003) 'Role of Volition and Complexity in Leadership', Master's thesis at McGill University

[14] Bruch, H. and Ghoshal, S., (2003), 'A Bias for Action', Harvard Business School Press, 2004

[15] Ach N., (1910), 'Über den Willensakt und das Temperament: Eine experimentelle Untersuchung (On the Act of the Will and Temperament: An Experimental Study)', Leipzig: Quelle and Meyer

unwavering, resolute engagement. Much later around 1980s, psychologists like Julius Kuhl[16] continued the good work on motivation, intention and volition and two others from the Munich University, Peter Gollwitzer and Heinz Heckhausen, came out with their famous concept of the Rubicon model[17] based on Ach's studies on *freier wille* (Fig. 10).

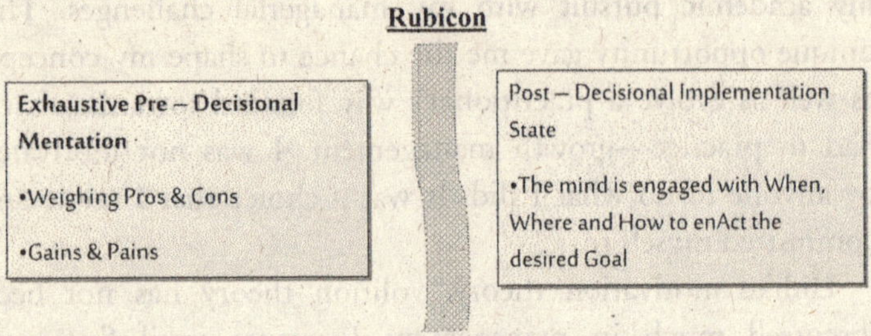

FIG. 10 – THE RUBICON

The Rubicon model draws inspiration from the idiom, 'Crossing the Rubicon' which means reaching a 'point of no return'. It is related to the legend about Julius Caesar when he with his legions decided to cross the river Rubicon on 11 January, 49 BC in his pursuit to regain Rome. One crosses the Rubicon in his mind when switching over mentally from a 'pre-decisional mentation' state (motivation arena) to a 'post-decisional implementation' (volition arena) state. Having

---

[16] Kuhl, J., (1985), 'Volitional Mediators of Cognition, Behaviour, Consistency: Self-regulatory Processes and Action Versus State Orientation,' in 'Action Control: From Cognition to Behavior,' eds. J. Kuhl and J. Beckmann (Berlin et al.: Springer, 1985), 101–128

[17] Gollwitzer, P.M., Heckhausen, H., and Ratajczak, H., (1990), 'From Weighing to Willing: Approaching a Change decision through pre- or post-decisional mentation,' Organizational Behaviour and Human Decision Processes 45 (1990)

crossed the Rubicon, one does not mentate anymore about the pros or cons but becomes focused only on the objective and the post implementation state of affairs. When making the decision to cross the Rubicon, Caesar had said, '*alea iacta est*' or 'The die is cast'.

Sumantra Ghoshal together with Heike Bruch while consulting Juergen Weber, the turnaround CEO of Lufthansa, found to their astonishment that only 10 percent of the project managers took purposive action to implement their projects despite all the hurdles that a turnaround normally throws up at a manager. For the rest, the problem was that fully knowing what they needed to do, they simply did not do it. The gap was not in knowledge, but between knowledge and action. They were positive about executing their projects but were not sure of the gains becoming a reality. They were all motivated to work for the national carrier but were yet apprehensive if the turnaround would really happen or not. They were still lingering in a pre-decisional mentation state. But the 10 percent had gone a decisive step further. Like Julius Caesar, these managers had crossed their personal Rubicons, from the arena of motivation to the arena of volition. It was the engagement of their will that gave them the power to overcome barriers, to deal with setbacks, to persevere through the high energy-sapping long journey from a wish or vision to its realization. These volitional managers were influential enough to become change agents (leaders) to help turnaround the ailing state run company into the successful listed giant we know today.

Motivation theory and its deficiency in instigating human behaviour to achieve remarkable achievements can be seen all across the organizational world. It remains a fact that all humans decide to do something with the expectation of gratifying their (self-perceived) unfulfilled needs and maximizing their value.

The stark difference between motivational and volitional engagement comes from the individual's mental state that plays on the situation one is faced with. Motivation is the arena of decision making while volition is the arena of implementation (Fig. 11). Motivation is about weighing pros and cons; a frantic search for intrinsic or extrinsic motivators that could outweigh the cons of a likely decision. Gollwitzer and Heckhausen (1990) called this arena of decision making as the state of *pre-decisional mentation.*

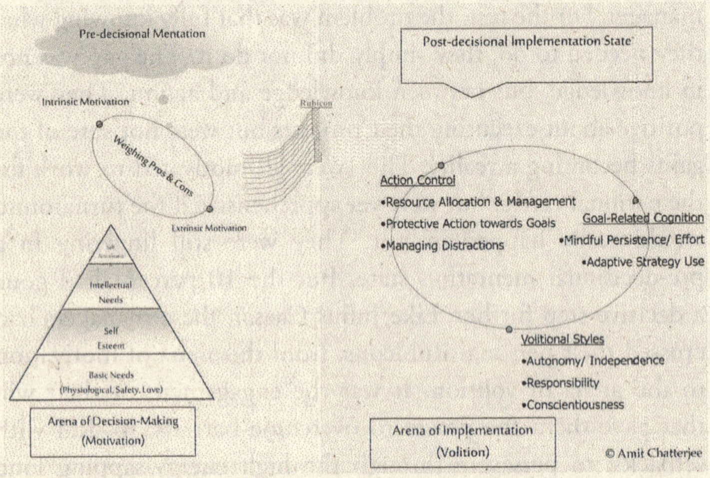

FIG. 11 – FROM THE MOTIVATION ARENA TO THE VOLITION ARENA

On the other side of the Rubicon, the volition arena is about clarity, the post-implementation state where we are immersed in the business of action control, managing distractions, goal related cognition, and volitional behaviour like autonomy, responsibility, and conscientiousness—all driven by the commitment to the chosen objective. The objective is what drives the decision to cross the Rubicon and not the gains that the decision maker may make if the objective is achieved. Motivation is a battle between the pros and cons that affects the decision maker, while volition is driven by the force of engagement with the objective that will fructify post the decision and actions.

In the words of Ghoshal and Bruch[18], '...motivation is a wish or a desire to do something—driven by intrinsic or extrinsic needs. Ultimately, motivation remains in the volatile state of wishing to engage, feeling attracted by certain opportunities or being tempted to act out certain behaviours. Both these extrinsic and intrinsic motivations are volatile in the sense that they are susceptible to changes. Extrinsic motivated behaviour is driven by the expectation of some reward; so there is always the danger that a more attractive opportunity will emerge, or that obstacles will come in the way and make the reward not worth the engagement. Intrinsically motivated managers experience interest and enjoy their activities; consequently there is always the danger that their interest will fade away or that their desires will change.

'Volition goes a decisive step further. It implies the commitment that only comes from a deep personal attachment to a certain intention... Volition is a robust force that is based on a conscious choice to make a concrete thing happen. Wilful managers are infected with an incurable need to produce certain results. They are not driven either by the expectation of a reward or by the joy of engaging in a certain activity. To the contrary, willpower enables managers to execute disciplined action even

[18] Ghoshal, S., and Bruch, H., (2003) 'Beyond Motivation to Volition: Unleashing the Power of Human Will', Sloan Management Review, Spring 2003

in situations when they lack the desire to do something... They do not expect to enjoy doing the work, or feel tempted by alternative opportunities.'

Now, the question that arises is, 'Do we need such volitional managers for every task, role, situation, or context in the day-to-day working of an organization?' The answer is, 'No, We don't.'

Managers driven by intrinsic or extrinsic motivators could be suited for for the meat of the daily work as long as they do not feel that their motivational interests are at risk. J. Kuhl (1985) found out that for routine tasks—when the goal is simple, actions necessary for their accomplishment are well practiced and relatively routine, and unexpected difficulties or obstacles are rare—motivation actually leads to action, even efficiency or higher productivity. Ralph Stacey calls these routine tasks as 'Simple Tasks'. These are not so difficult to manage in the short-term.

Normal managerial work, however, is not necessarily about the linear, the smooth cause and effect kind of activity. Henry Mintzberg[19] (1973) has consistently explained that managerial jobs are often not routine, and 'Managers have to pursue multiple and often conflicting goals, many of which require persistent action over long periods of time. Their work context tends to be fragmented, with high levels of both uncertainty and opposition'. As a practitioner, I found most managers' lives as per Mintzberg's description albeit interspersed with doses of routine or simple tasks like task planning, monitoring, analysing, signing paperwork, or reporting. Convincing stakeholders, decision making, visioning for the future, meetings, resolving conflicts, inspiring others, mentoring, or change management

---

[19] Mintzberg, H., (1973), 'The Nature of Managerial Work,' (New York: Harper Collins, 1973)

are managerial tasks that needs volitional engagement, or 'volitionals', driven by longer-term objectives.

Hence, a management culture that depends densely on motivation theory can manage the short-term but the jewels of the long-term—innovation, ethics, vision, uncertainty, opposition, hurdles of the unknown, entry barriers, competitive advantage, or the constituents of the SPG (sustained profitable growth)—will remain elusive unless we create room for volitional engagement. The above 'jewels of the long-term' are the playground of those who constitute the leadership of an organization. A management that is driven by motivation theory alone cannot select, nurture, groom, and manage volitionals.

A management that facilitates volitional engagement creates a nursery for leadership and paves the way towards SPG.

A discussion on volition would be incomplete without mentioning the risks of volitional engagement. The risk primarily lies in the very strength of volitional engagement, that of precluding any other alternative. Fig. 11 shows the characteristic of a volitionally-engaged manager who is focused on the objective and implementation unmindful of his possibility of gains or pains. Such a person runs the risk of being oblivious of what is happening around him. At times, it may become evident that the goal pursued is going to meet with failure or a major contextual change due to uncontrollable or unforeseen factors necessitates disengagement of the volitional pursuit. It becomes very difficult and painful for volitional managers to do that as in their minds they had completely precluded any other alternative.

Building stopping rules through review and respect mechanisms is most important. Unlike motivated managers, volitional managers or leaders cannot be instructed to disengage and re-engage with some other task. They need to themselves come to a conclusion that a pursued goal may have become redundant and hence needs to be disengaged with. They need to themselves build in the review mechanism to monitor the context and allow their own cognizance to come to the disengagement decision. The disengagement with the volitional pursuit is made easier when the pursuit is subservient in their minds to the larger purpose that hooks their will and emotions. A manager passionate about contributing to the growth of her enterprise would find it easier to disengage from a project that she is leading when a review mechanism brings out the fact that the project needs to be abandoned as the context has changed and pursuing it would not lead to the growth of the enterprise.

Risk also lies in managing people with habits of volitional pursuit in their foundation stage of life. It is difficult to engage them with tasks that are important but not chosen or accepted by their subconscious. Such people suffer from 'ego depletion' (Baumeister[20] et al., 1998) as they cannot fill up their energy banks from normal routine tasks and end up depleting their ego or energy. Managers with volitional habits are used to doing things when drawn by the overarching purpose that they identify with. They are used to making choices and decisions on what they have to do. When they are asked to take up a task or do something without knowing why it has to be done, they do not feel any need to do it. If they are forced to do such tasks on instructions from their seniors without being party to the decision why it has to be done, their ego is 'depleted' and feel completely drained. On the other hand, Volitionals get energy from tasks that lie in their complexity zones, characterised by

---

[20] Baumeister, R., Bratslavsky, E., Muraven, M., and Tice, D.; (1998), 'Ego depletion: Is the active self a limited resource?' Journal of Personality and Social Psychology, 74(5), 1252–1265

uncertainty and/or lack of agreement. In these situations, they make their own choices when crossing their Rubicons and suffer no ego depletion. Instead they feel no pain or lack of energy even if they are working without any rest or respite. They do not need any 'motivation' from anybody. They generate their own energy from their volitional pursuits.

Can you motivate a composer to compose great music? Try motivating a parent to do good parenting; have you seen anybody motivating a business manager to double the business in three to five years? Try motivating a manager to develop great leaders in his or her team. Those who have succeeded in the above, have done it only through volitional engagement. The volitional arena truly lies beyond anybody's expectations.

4

The Narcissist

Although Maslow did not talk about narcissism in his paper on human motivation, narcissism would form an intrinsic part of the Self-esteem needs in Maslow's hierarchy. This is a motivational trait based on the pathological development of an individual. It is dependent on the unfulfilled need of the individual for praise or approval in its childhood and is manifested in adulthood as a hunger for power and prestige (Kohut[21], 1971). Narcissistic needs are known to have propelled many a manager to top leadership positions (Kernberg[22], 1979) as the accoutrements of a top management position offer the highest possibility to a narcissist in an organization to gratify his or her need for power and fame.

We have seen in the earlier chapters the impotency of pecuniary motivators to develop leadership worthy of 'remarkable achievements'. We have also seen that this creates a perennial pursuit of unfulfilled self-esteem needs and may make man oblivious to higher needs like intellectual or self-actualization needs.

---

[21] Kohut, H., (1971), 'The Analysis of the Self', New York: International Universities Press

[22] Kernberg, O., (1979), 'Regression in Organizational Leadership'; Psychiatry, 42, 29–39

A narcissist being motivated by pecuniary motivators is like holding a matchstick to a long fuse connected to an ammunition dump. As money or money's worth are the easiest instruments to buy prestige and power, the narcissist will not only love to capture such a position but be like a predator whose appetite has been whetted and he will do everything to maintain his position. The only reason he would give it away will be when a change in the context makes him feel that his need for prestige, fame, and power is at big risk of being gratified. Another reason could be when an alternative host context lures him away with a promise for greater prestige, fame, and power.

Researchers like Kets de Vries and Miller (1984)[23] have pointed out that a certain dose of narcissism is necessary for Managers to function effectively, '... Among those who show limited narcissistic tendencies we find those who are very talented and capable of making great contributions to society. Those who gravitate to the extremes, however, give narcissism its pejorative reputation.' They also observed that a person who in more normal circumstances might have led an ordinary life, has used expectations imposed on him as a child as a basis for excellence. But, this is the excellence of the loner, the autocrat, not necessarily that of a leader.

The narcissist is quite a puritan in his choices. He is not motivated by the pecuniary benefits per se. As we have noted above, he is only in the pursuit of prestige, fame, and power. He may lead a flamboyant lifestyle as this anoints him with prestige and gives him the power over others, but he could yet be saintly in his disinterest in comparative supremacy. While

---

[23] Kets de Vries, M. F. R. and Miller, D., (1984),'Narcissism and Leadership: An Object relations perspective', Working Paper, INSEAD, No. 85/19

he will be abrasive and reject you when he is thwarted in his pursuits that he goes after with a vengeance, he is not one to go after his opposition with vindictiveness. The narcissist can be quite noble once his thirst for fame and power are relatively quenched. The narcissist can handle simultaneous pursuit of intellectual needs and self-actualization as development on these fronts may also add to his fame, prestige, and power.

The danger lies in the fact that a narcissistic personality may quite easily be mistaken for a volitionally engaged person by most. Their manifestations at work could be quite similar, although the behavioural aspects may differ. A narcissist would appear to be as 'purpose' driven as a volitional. Their obsessive pursuit of the goal and ability to discard any distraction could be equally intensive. But, deeper down, the fundamental difference lies in the narcissist pursuing the purpose or goal for the personal outcomes in the form of fame and power, whereas the volitional is driven only by the purpose.

Kets de Vries and Miller brought out from their research the pathological development of different varieties of narcissism as shown in Fig. 12. It shows the relationship between parenting, behaviour, symptoms, and manifestation in organizational context for three different types of narcissistic managers. Their work can be quite helpful to differentiate between narcissists and volitionals.

The narcissist's behavioural manifestations are seen in the following types of reactions. The most important aspect of this behaviour is that the narcissist is normally not conscious of the manifestations; hence if you are observant, you would be able to spot the narcissist quite easily:

- Denial—The narcissist refuses to acknowledge the difference between the actual and the self-perceived

Ideal Varieties of Narcissism

	Reactive	**Self-Deceptive**	**Constructive**	
Early Object Relations	Rejecting, Unresponsible parenting Absence of secure attachment	Overburdening Parenting Absence of secure attachment	"Good enough" Care Sense of Acceptance	(Etiology)
Defense reactions	Pervasive/ Severe Frequent	Splitting/ Projective Identification Idealisation/ Devaluation	Rare Mild, Infrequent	
Symptomatology Entitlement	Exhibitionism, Grandiosity Ruthlessness, Coldness,	Lack of Empathy, Machiavellianism Fear of Failure, "Ideal Hungry" Preoccupation (with own needs)	Sense of Humor, Creativity Self-Confidence, Ambition, Stubborn/ Pride	
	(Want to Dominate)	**(Want to be loved)**	**(Want to achieve)**	
Manifestation in Organizational Functioning				
Leadership	Transforming Orientation Expelling Mode; wants Sycophants Cruel Task Master Enraged by Criticism	Transactional Orientation Binding Mode; Likes non-critical subordinates; Diplomatic Hurt by criticism	Transforming/Transactional Reciprocal Mode Meritocratic; Inspirational, Mentor Learns from Criticism	
Decision Making	Major, Risk-laden Consults No One Crushes Opponents Uses Scapegoats Never admits defeat	Conservative, Risk Averse Overcautious Consults too many Lacks Reslove	Consultative in Information gathering Independent in decision making Inner Directed	

FIG. 12 – IDEAL VARIETIES OF NARCISSISM

Ideal Self; denial of the actual is an unconscious method of coping with his internal conflict, anxiety, emotional distress or pain, leading to increased confidence and feelings of invulnerability.

- Rationalization—He attempts to justify or find reasons for unacceptable behaviour or feelings; presents them in a form consciously tolerable and acceptable; indulges in self-deception to make what is consciously repugnant appear more creditable.
- Self-aggrandizement—manifests a tendency to overestimate his merits, abilities, and accomplishments as an unconscious wish for fulfilment or gratification of his need for fame and power; he is prone to fantasies accompanied by extreme self-absorption, exhibitionism, claims to uniqueness, and a sense of invulnerability.
- Attributional Egotism—a tendency to offer explanations for events that are self-serving; attributes favourable outcomes to causes, to the self and unfavourable outcomes to external causes—helps preserve his self-esteem.
- Sense of Entitlement—A strong belief in his right to exploit others as a compensation for having been deprived of attachment in his foundation days. He is unable to empathise with the feelings of others and entertains shallow interpersonal relationships. The Narcissist cannot live without an admiring audience. His apparent freedom from family ties and institutional constraints does not free him to stand alone. It contributes to his insecurity!
- Anxiety—Ability to live with anxiety and use the same to unleash positive energy.

It is anxiety that makes the narcissist find common identity with the volitional. Both personalities are friends of anxiety and unconsciously use anxiety to further their ends. Barring anxiety, all other characteristics of a narcissist as detailed above can be easily observed in real time environments as a marked differentiator to the volitionally engaged.

Having discussed the drivers for a narcissist and his behavioural manifestations, I will go into three paradigms about a narcissist in organizational life and discuss the management options for both a manager who has to manage a narcissist and for the narcissist himself:

1. The narcissist as a leader

Let us revisit the basis for 'remarkable achievements' expected from leadership. They are ethics, empathy, creativity, innovation, greatness, development of other conscientious leaders, social responsibility, and finally doing everything to ensure sustained profitable growth (SPG). The narcissist can bring in values like creativity and innovation but may not be so committed to other deeper values like ethics, empathy, development of conscientious leaders, and social responsibility. The narcissist does succeed in creating remarkable achievements that suit the comparative mode of organizational hierarchy (refer to Fig. 8) but he does not really work for the long-term goal of the organization in creating SPG. Hence, the tenure of a narcissist in an organization is limited to certain short-term contexts or achievements.

Certain managements or boards have knowingly used narcissists in leadership functions to drive dramatic change particularly to yank an enterprise out of staid historical ghettos or from 'survival mode' to a 'comparative mode'. This works but finally the narcissist has to leave the enterprise as he brings the enterprise to teetering heights of activity and risks that are not sustainable. I read an article in a German newspaper about what a narcissist left in his wake. The article was titled *'Mr XYZ left a burnt garden after three years as the CEO…'* As the garden needs to be brought back to life while the paradigm has been changed for keeps, the best suited successor to a narcissist leadership would be a more methodical, disciplined but consolidating type of leadership.

2. Dealing with a narcissist

The reactive narcissistic is better avoided in normal life. Sadly, such people are the most difficult to form any kind of relationship with as they are too acute in all their six manifestations, from denial to anxiety. They are better suited for solo roles that give them enough prestige and power. With more and more enterprises becoming a knowledge organization, there are not many such roles in an organization anymore. Other than the entrepreneur who leaves the management of the enterprise to others or the very rare specialist role, a reactive narcissist cannot be anymore an organization man or woman.

On the other hand, the constructive narcissist can be a boon for most leadership positions. The great opportunity lies in the constructive narcissist working with a volitional engagement to the objectives of the enterprise. The deceptive narcissist for me is clearly not a fit for any leadership position as he would never be able to take decisions as he looks for appeasing the powers to be. Even if he takes some decisions he would not be able to stand by them when faced with implementation hurdles.

3. How do I handle my narcissistic tendencies?

The weaknesses of a narcissist are sensitivity to criticism, poor listening skills, lack of empathy, dislike for mentoring, and an intense desire to compete to gain fame and power.

The good news for a narcissist comes from his knowledge about the pathological nature behind these tendencies. It may be temporarily turbulent for the emotional state of the individual, but there is no better way for a narcissist to handle himself than knowing himself as best as he can. This reminds me of a 1994 Jack Nicholson movie named *The Wolf*, where he comes to know about his dangerous tendencies and decides to seek help from experts to protect the woman he loves and himself from his own weakness.

The more reactive narcissist I am, faster I need to seek help. Help can come in the way of someone I trust who I 'authorize' to criticize or stop me when I fly off the handle in my manifestations. Help can be sought by having what some may call as a 'side-kick' who shields the narcissist from others and vice versa. Of course, to have a side-kick who will not exploit such a confidence in itself could be a great risk. But, narcissists are quite sharp and deep in their understanding of people, even if they cannot openly practice empathy. Help can be in the form of reflection time built by decision to develop a forced habit to check intuitive reactions before making them public or getting them vetted by your trusted side-kick.

I am a practising manager and may not have the expertise of a practising psychotherapist. But, I am sure help can also be sought from such specialists to overcome the ghosts from one's past that cast the narcissistic shadows in our adult life. Thankfully, most individuals do not fall at the edges of a statistical bell curve and can manage themselves quite well, once they are aware of the science behind our manifestations.

It is worthwhile to remember that like most things in life, too much of narcissism can be a stiff challenge but without a pinch of narcissism we could be lost in oblivion.

I am profoundly aware that theoretical discussions on topics like motivation, volition, narcissism, etc. are not exactly the best pastimes for busy managers. But, it is no different than learning any other science needed by a professional to excel in their professional domains. I hope that the writing treatment I could offer on these topics provides enough bias for action to my readers.

PART 4

The Leader's Arena

John Van Maanen, one of the dons of Organizational Studies, said, 'Culture in itself is not visible, but is made visible only through its representation'. What better instruments of representation can an enterprise have other than its leadership across the length and breadth of the organization? So, let us dive in into what leaders do.

This part offers six chapters differing in their bouquets but with the lingering taste of the Practising Manager's Growth Mantra. As in a wine tasting ceremony, the intention behind this collection is not to offer a textbook promise of completeness, but to make you enjoy the variety and experiences in the domain of leadership or management.

The Leadership Wine List

- *Stress and Leadership*
- *Risk, Leadership and Management*
- *Strategy and Leadership*
- *Conflict and Leadership*
- *The Followers*
- *Redundancy and the Growth Engine*

The chapters were triggered by contexts and reflections at different periods over the last few years. The interplay of the managerial science from the earlier part is not a coincidence, but a proof of application of the same in real time management thinking and action.

1

Stress and Leadership

'...yet, a decade of organizational delayering, de-staffing, restructuring, and reengineering has produced employees who are more exhausted than empowered, more cynical than self-renewing. Worse still, in many companies only marginal managerial attention—if that—is focused on the problems of employee capability or motivation.'

GRATTON & GHOSHAL (2003)[24]

Why lead, if that leads to stress?
Why not just be led?

Stress has reportedly become an epidemic, almost endemic, to organizations and companies.

That people in leadership functions suffer from stress is a refrain we hear day in and day out in the organizational world. Volumes have been written about the workload and methodologies to manage the same. Stress management workshops and trainers have increased their turnover and

[24] Gratton, L., and Ghoshal, S., (2003), 'Competing on Personal Human Capital: New Ethos for the "Volunteer" employee', European Management Journal. February, 2003

price tags all over the world but the disease shows no sign of abatement.

The leadership tribe keeps pumping the adrenaline with incessant meetings, emails, tele/video/internet conferences, dinners and smart phones. Sometimes I tend to believe that the smart phone technology has been funded by the healthcare/pharmaceutical industry to maintain an unending supply of patients for *their* growth appetites. And the social media acts as a compliment to augment the supply by keeping the busy managers/leaders even busier by making them indulge in *'thumbolysis'* on their touch screens. Gurus of emotional quotient management have gone hoarse in vain while age-old techniques of meditation or ayurvedic rejuvenation packages have started selling at premiums threatening the established bastions of perfumery czars. The marriage of stress and leadership seems to be the only marriage that does not appear to be afflicted by the supreme disease of the affluent society—divorce.

Therefore, we need to pause a while and relook at the etiology of this leadership disease named stress. There has to be some motivator, or a brace at least, that catapults us from our relatively comfortable couches (pre-leadership positions) into the exposed terrain of leadership functions—be it in a team, company, or in the social or political arena. We need to go into the root causes and ask the question:

What makes one yearn for or accept responsibilities in an organization that requires them to lead?

- Is it the perks and the pay check of leadership positions that makes one lead?
- Is it the fear of being cast away from the mainstream that makes one lead?

- Is it the lure of power and fame that makes one take on the lead mantle?
- Is it the compulsion to measure up to the expectations of those in whose eyes one can't just afford to look small?
- Or a combination of the above unfulfilled needs?

After all, we are all prisoners of Mr Maslow's motivational hierarchy of needs. Spurred by any of the above unfulfilled needs springs the desire to take on the leadership roles and lo and behold, in no time we are in the business of managing stress.

There are some people, however, who take on similar roles not merely driven by the above needs, but because they envision the purpose of the role themselves and want to actualize the same. They are not looking at what they will get, acquire, be known for, or hoard once the role goal is fulfilled under their charge. They are fuelled by the passion of one day seeing their goals or purpose mature into reality. They are the guys who find time to not only do what they can do, but also to fire up those around them and make them as fired up about the purpose or goals as they themselves are. Their teams stick to them, their families stand by them and their management supports them as everybody around them, gets infected by their passion and love for the purpose that they want to lead towards and fulfil.

On the other hand, for *Maslow's prisoners*, the personal gains are the reason one leads for, while for the latter group—I call them the *Volitionals*—they lead driven by the purpose, the goals required of their roles. The Volitionals approach the purpose as their *Karma* while the Maslow's prisoners count their chickens even before the hens are fertile.

The Volitionals do not feel any stress on account of their work as they are hooked by a higher purpose which drives them internally. Maslow's prisoners get tired due to the hard work they have to put in and keep looking at the distance they have to go before few or one of their motivational needs gets fulfilled. At times, they succumb to the work pressure and accept even a partial fulfilment of their needs as the work was always toil for them. They did not work to fulfil the objectives of their roles, but for their personal gains. When we are in the motivation arena (Fig. 11), one always analyses the pros and cons, fervently calculating the gains versus the pain one has to take for the same. When the pain become too painful to realize the maximum gains, we rationalize in our minds and walk away with reduced gain and avoid any more pain. So, the Maslow's prisoners end up in a *'satisfactory underperformance'* loop. On the other hand, the volitionals don't even know when to stop and more often than not, end up over-performing.

The Maslow's prisoners know that they underperformed in their leadership roles and cannot justify to their own why they sacrificed other things in their lives and end up in a double whammy of a guilty conscience—both on their professional and personal fronts. Thus flows the aetiology of stress; it comes from the punctured psyche and not from the overworked physique or the workload.

The volitionals also go through a lot of physical stress, but do not suffer from guilt. Their role tends to be their life and their close ones know that and hence support them. The satisfactory underperformers live a life of compromise on all fronts and hence look for work–life balance, whereas for the volitionals, work is a subset of life, not a competitor. They can make mistakes about their priorities and be disappointed, but they will not suffer from emotional stress. They have a chance to reflect later and fix their future priorities but they won't join the lamentation camp and brood over their half-filled cups of work and life. The volitionals can look back on something done well and something not done at all—they have no half problem in their lives. They have either a solution that they are intensely working on till it is consummated or they have a problem that they have not addressed yet.

Hence, leadership work or purpose of work is never the etiological causation for stress. It is the self-perception of one's unfulfilled needs or the attitude to life that makes one hunt for purpose in their work (a subset of their lives) that can either become the virus causing the disease or the vaccine that prevents the infection.

A life spent with the purpose of topping up 'unfulfilled needs' may be normal behaviour for the human race and Maslow was right for sure; but this is a life about fulfilling expectations, even if they are our own. Such a life can never be bereft of stress.

Instead, we need to try to lead our lives to fulfil goals and purposes, however small they maybe. In each leadership role we are blessed to occupy, we have the choice to design our work purpose, to dream what best can be done, and aim to actualize such dreams. We may have so many dreams and only a few may mature. The few that mature are enough to lead a life worth living and be free of stress. As volitionals, we will be creating so many successes for ourselves at work, at home, and if we are lucky even in the society we live off. That is a life lived beyond expectations.

2

Risk, Leadership, and Management

Between management and the future, lies the *grand canyon of Risks*. It is across this canyon of risks, beyond the boundaries of our today's expectations that our *Karma* lies—the long term or larger purpose of our life. It is Leadership that keeps throwing the rope of visioning across this canyon, till it hooks onto a purpose and holds. The rope of vision snaps taut in no time as the leader crosses the Rubicon or the canyon of risks in his mind. Immersed in a post-decisional implementation state, the volitionally engaged leader embarks on a risky journey to attain its purpose and fructify the vision it is hooked on to. His opponents stare in consternation and his followers break into a roar of applause as he takes the first steps across the yawning chasm. As cold sweat trickles down the spine, the leadership mind steels its resolve and shuts itself to the uproar it leaves in its wake...ramrod straight, taut as a string, and alert as a cat on the prowl, the leader puts its feet on the stretched tightrope, unmindful of failure.

The body and each cell in it are tuned to all elements of nature. It senses the tiniest of change around and adapts to the same. It hears no adulation, it expects no rewards; the achievement of the goal is its only persuasion. No distraction can deter him, no aspiration is big enough than the objective driving his volition. Maslow's prisoners hate him, hold him in awe, and perspire while the leader carries on across the tightrope oblivious of all emotions. All his senses are focussed on that point at the end of the rope where lies his reward, the actualization of his dream, the purpose of his existence.

Risk mitigation, risk management, and risk alleviation have become the buzzwords for the managerial creed. Management naturally breeds risk aversion. It curbs recruitment of risk friendly personnel. It dithers from developing a culture that develops risk appetite. The organization becomes a haven of safety, rules, SOPs, and deviation management. Today is great; we need to sustain the same and not taking any risks becomes the credo. Analysts, statistical averages, and executives set up their tent right at the centre of Mr Gauss' bell curve. Anyone showing tendencies to drift towards the extremes is declared a pariah.

The controlling head sits atop the bell curve and keeps a hawk's eye on any flutter beyond the expected. Living within expectations and strolling around the known terrains makes life akin to living on the organizational *Riviera*. Under Gauss' median tent, life is about routine, efficiency, productivity, and stability. Everyone knows each other, everyone and everything are predictable. All will continue forever; we are sailing in a yacht on *Lake Placid*. Just do it; yours is not to think, but to keep at it!

But, risk management need not mean risk aversion or avoidance. It could mean taking risks that do not kill the organization but when successful, will put the enterprise or the organization into a different realm, will raise the bar, create entry barriers, and deliver competitive advantage.

But, who will take the risks? Could it be those who are obsessed with 'topping up their unfulfilled needs' of today? Or those who have been immunised against risk taking by their controllers? Or those who are busy running Rome—executing assignments with strict deliverables?

The challenge lies in selection of people and the proportion of volitionals in the management team at different levels and groups. The management needs to ensure a culture that recruits, nurtures, and allows adequate number of volitionals to scour the horizon, to cast their ropes across the craters around. Even a column of ants have volitionals who make sorties that discover the ingredients for their long-term survival.

Non-volitionals or Maslow's prisoners can act as speed breakers, provide safety kits, build alarm systems, press the brake lever, and run the SOPs. But, if one does not have volitionals in the team, there will be no risk taken, no entry barriers built, no competitive advantage generated and hence, no 'sustained profitable growth'.

The good news is that most, if not all, individuals possess a mix of volitional and need fulfilment drivers. Managers who understand the significance of breeding leadership consciously steer the drivers as an optimal mix, both at the individual and organizational levels. They do not need to work so hard on their own. That is how the unhappy marriage between stress and managers can be sought to be annulled.

Since each individual is the carrier of both need fulfilment and volitional drivers, the choice of being prisoners of Maslow's hierarchy of needs or unleashing their volitional energies in pursuit of chosen purposes does remain with the individual. Hence, any individual per se can practice an optimal mix of their own drivers and that is where lies the development potential of each organization, man, or woman.

For the management of any team or organization, the development potential lies in their choosing and nurturing individuals who can unleash their volitional energies. Managers can design the contours of roles and contexts for their team members to allow them to cast their leadership ropes across the canyon of risks. On the other side, when motivating an individual, the big risk lies in what is realistic as 'unfulfilled needs' that the individual may expect to be met. Most of Maslow's needs are real to the perceiver, but they cannot be fulfilled in the short term. It is the task of a manager to make their team members embrace realities and not live in wishful fantasies.

Management needs to empathize with the self-perceived trajectory of individuals regarding their major motivators or unfulfilled needs. They need to have the confidence of being transparent and helping the individuals to match their perceptions of expectations to realities and potentials in the short term. The long term is okay for the volitionals as they are driven by the vision or the purpose and not just by their unfulfilled needs. Therefore, the volitionally engaged are there for the long haul, as long as it takes to actualise the purpose of work or life. For those motivationally engaged with the hope of gratifying their unfulfilled needs, the work that they have to do becomes a toil, the pain that they have to go through to make the gains. They are not there for the long haul and instead look for the shortest milestones and the rewards attached to them.

The biggest risk lies in whether the management itself is driven by volitional engagement or their short-term motivational aspirations. They will never be able to tap the volitional drivers in their team members and breed doers instead of leaders who would be willing to take any risks for the long term. Risk also lies in channelizing the volitional energies, in building organizational traffic lights for the unstoppables—the volitionals. Risk lies in recruiting the reactive narcissists (can be easily mistaken for volitionals) whose prime motivation comes from fulfilling their need for fame and power. Risk lies in non-conformance between values manifested through decisions, actions, and behaviour of the management and the accepted (not declared alone) values of the organization. Risk lies in curbing the volitional energies of many in different parts of the organization when asked to conform, comply, and merely perform for short-term deliverables.

An organization not only develops success and sustainability when its management invests in balancing risk and leadership with efficiency and effectiveness, it also offers a happy and vibrant life for all the employees in an organization.

> *Management is the kitchen that produces a delicious meal, where Leadership is the Chef hooked by a purpose across the canyon of risks that adds the fragrance and taste to make it go beyond expectations!*

3

Strategy and Leadership

'It is up to us to decide what it means to be a successful Human Being. Nothing happens unless You make it happen. As a leader everything is your responsibility, because You could have chosen otherwise.'

PETER KOESTENBAUM

Strategy has something to do with leadership. Could one think about a leader without a strategy? What is she leading towards? Whom is she leading—the followers? How does the leader explain the strategy to her followers?

Let us then dwell upon what is this strategy that one should have in order to lead. Is it just a dream, a goal, an objective, or is it one of these or a combination of some or all of these? Many years back, I was fortunate to participate in the post-modern management program called *impm* evolved under the great Henry Mintzberg and Jonathan Gosling. In one of the initial lectures where Henry was in his element on the topic of strategy, he squiggled different shapes and arrows to explain his thoughts and concepts. One of the shapes he drew was an umbrella with the word 'vision' written across the umbrella's protective cover held aloft by analysis, planning, and implementation. It got imprinted on my mind as it made sense to me (I was

41 then). Later when I taught a course on Leadership and Change Management at IIM Bangalore, I wanted to explain the beauty of Henry's strategy umbrella, but struggled with how to communicate the word 'vision' to a bunch of budding young managers. It could not be surmised as just dreams, else we would be left dreaming with nothing to act upon.

I thought for a bit and came up with another word which was more action oriented—possibilities. I define possibilities as those things that we are *not* doing, but which *can* be done with existing resources including knowledge, and time. All one needs to do to identify the possibilities in any context is ask the following questions belw:

- Are we doing everything that we can do in the context we are in today? The answer would always be—No.
- What are those few things we can do additionally? One would always find some—these are the possibilities.

Since these possibilities can be acted upon without any additional resources, action can be initiated and growth can ensue. Actions while executing possibilities would create additional resources for the future and that could become the fuel for actualizing tomorrow, the dreams of today. Hence, dreams are such things that we can only work upon when we have created additional resources.

The sum total of possibilities and dreams is what equals vision:
Vision = Possibilities + Dreams

In the real world, even possibilities cannot be acted upon without adequate analysis followed by planning and implementation, while dreams need to be researched and analysed too before one can start planning for them. Activities like analysis, planning, and even implementation are very important and need to be done by experts in their respective domains. These activities fall squarely in the domain of the manager, while when the manager is carving out the vision, she is in leadership mode. When all the above—vision, analysis, planning, implementation—have been clearly penned down in good detail, the entire workout can be called the strategy. The equation can be formulated as under:

$$Strategy = Analysis * f(Vision)^{Planning} * Implementation$$

The crux of strategy lies in the vision, without which there is nothing to analyse, plan, or implement. Therefore, the first stage of leadership activity is about creating the vision or coming up with the possibilities and dreams in the context. The context can be about a team, a function, a division, a company, or just a life and what the leader envisages it to be in the future. A manager, whether managing a small team or a multi-billion dollar company, has to have a strategy. A manager having a strategy without a vision would be like a headless chicken running around in circles ending up with paralysis through analysis. A manager who can build a vision is a leader; if she can execute the strategy well but cannot build a vision, she is a great manager; if she can do both, build the vision as well as execute the strategy smartly, she is a star *leader–manager*.

Who would not want to be the star leader–manager? Maybe there are some saintly people without a pinch of narcissism. Now, it is important to think what motivates a manager to be a leader; to have the capacity, the mindset, to envision the future of his team, function, division, or a company. Can you motivate or incentivise a person to dream or have a vision?

No! Leadership is not the business of people who need to be motivated!

You cannot motivate an author to write a wonderful book, a scientist to invent something, or a prime minister to have a vision for his country. *A leader is volitionally engaged. Period.*

The mindset to think of possibilities or dream about the future stems from a few basic principles of leadership thinking and behaviour. The leader *decides* to do something about the situation. The leader *chooses* to explore the development potential of the context. The leader does not need to be motivated or assigned a task. The leader is driven by being in a post-decisional implementation state—that is where her mind conjures the vision of what her team or company should be like in some years; that is what gives her the ability to vividly describe how it would be, what are we doing once the vision is achieved; that is what enables the leader to envisage what kind of resources would be necessary and finally what kind of leadership would be required to lead the entity at that stage. All this is a mental game, a play on the ability to dream of greatness, sustainability, and growth in the long term. No expectation of fulfilling unfulfilled needs in the short term can make a manager transform into a leader. All this is possible when the manager is hooked by the purpose of growth for her domain of responsibility. *Only the volitional can go that far, obsessed by the purpose and passionate about the execution.*

And when one needs to decide and do something about a context, the context is not about tasks where one is certain about what or how they have to be done or where different stakeholders are already in agreement that such tasks have to be done. Decisions are needed when one is at crossroads. Vision is paramount to make others buy into the purpose of taking up such tasks. It is about uncertainty and lack of agreement or complexity as defined in the Stacey's Matrix (Fig. 2) where leadership is necessary. This is where options stare at you and you can see them only when you are looking for possible ways to fructify your vision. This is where you need to make a choice amongst the possible options based upon which option could lead you and your team to your purpose. This is possible when you are volitionally engaged with the vision.

Therefore, leadership is what is required in the complexity zone while managerial working is needed in situations stacked with relative certainty and agreement, where one does not have to decide or choose, only execute as per agreed or accepted procedures, quality, and achieve zero defect results. This is the arena of expertise, efficiency, and high efficacy—of set targets and results.

Volition is the personality trait that flourishes in complexity—in the realm of uncertainty, ambiguity, conflict, chaos, and risks. Every managerial role in an organization has the scope for its relative doses of complexity, when the manager faces more than one option to go forward and has to make a choice. If the choice is made based on motivational engagement, it may lead to the purpose only when the chances of securing the manager's unfulfilled needs are quite high. But more often than not, managerial life throws up challenges that do not have a high degree of security of success as they need to be steered through many a hurdle and an opposition. When driven by motivators with low chances of bearing fruit, managers can at the best end up with satisfactory underperformance accepting compromises both in the their work results as well as their expected gains. Therefore, the motivationally engaged could fit the personality trait of a *great* short-term manager.

How many managers does an organization need merely for the short term?

Fortunately, nature always gives us an option to find a way—once we are looking for it. Most people have a decent mix of both the personality traits, that of being driven more by motivational engagement or volitional engagement. And thankfully, the mix is lopsided, due to random influences from our formative years and the environment under which we get conditioned in our adult lives. If only one could identify the trait mix and depute people with a pronounced trait fitting the context, we would be *vrooming towards Xanadu in no time!* As leaders or managers who wish to act as leaders, we could choose the option of conditioning our people including ourselves to develop the volitional trait more. One easy way is not to use the motivational baton or succumb to it!

If 'running Rome' is the task, let us find people with more of the motivational trait and when we need to 'transform Rome' let us go for the more volitional types.

> *The challenge lies with the latter choice to be made, as most managers driven by their narcissistic needs, sub-consciously expect leadership thinking or volitional traits only off themselves, while others with these traits in the organization either wither away or away they wander.*

4

Conflict and Leadership

'Managerial jobs, however, are often not routine. Managers have to pursue multiple and often conflicting goals, many of which require persistent action over long periods of time. Their work context tends to be fragmented, with high levels of both uncertainty and opposition.'

HENRY MINTZBERG

Leaders create conflicts, while managers have to manage them.

A few years ago as I sat preparing for a lecture on leadership I had been invited for, my barely teenaged kids went around my study inspecting what I was up to. To engage them, I asked, 'What does a leader do?' My daughter chirped instantaneously to her elder brother's amazement, 'They decide and act'.

I could not disagree. Leaders do take decisions and initiate actions. A decision becomes necessary only when action cannot be continued until a choice has been made. In real life, individuals, teams, organizations, or companies are at crossroads more often than they realize. Every crossroad situation is complexity for the leadership involved and hence an opportunity. The 'unknown or uncertain' part may come from the lack of knowledge (experience) or due to different opinions about the way forward. Crossroads also brings out the leader in us as someone has to make a choice or decide before any action can be taken. In a group, the individuals who push for a certain pathway are leaders in their individual capacities but the person who takes the final decision to go 'that way' carries the onus of being the leader of the group. But that is merely the beginning of the leadership role. The moment a decision is made, there are at least two sides—one who either understand or accept the decision and the other who do not understand or still believe their way would be better. And, wham, you have a conflict.

Are conflicts good or bad? Like chocolates, strategies, or movies, conflict too can lead to good or bad consequences. But unlike chocolates, strategies, or movies that have ingredients potent for good or bad results, conflicts are just 'envelopes of opportunities'. What goes into this envelope depends on the leadership among the conflicting sides. As the first phase of the conflict evolves, there is great opportunity for finding a wonderful recipe to fill into this empty envelope of conflict.

Good Conflict—An Envelope of Opportunity

Once a decision has been made, it simply means change of status quo. Some would agree and some would not. This is normal. This phase starts with arguments or debates in an organization between people who are required to work together for the larger objectives of the same organization. An individual argues or debates, when there is still *faith* in the reason why he has to do something or work with another individual. People on either side of the conflict still *trust* the purpose of working together and hence would debate with full conviction about their way. They *believe* that they need to put their point of view and someone is listening sincerely. Such debates arise from either side having a different set of facts that they build their thesis upon. These interactions—arguments and debates—could still become pregnant with something great as a final outcome as long as the basis for their faith, trust, and belief remains the same—the *purpose* of doing something together.

In such good conflicts, the arguments or debates are normally about what I prefer to label as the 'inanimate' topics related to tasks (what), processes (how), resources (with what) including skills. Now, these whats, hows, or with whats are normally in the domain of *knowns* for a team or an organization. Decisions on such inanimate topics relate to the expertise and experience of the manager for which she is responsible and thereby has the authority to decide. Normally, conflicts on such inanimate topics get settled under the weight of domain practice and organizational hierarchy.

In these inanimate conflicts, the potential for the best decision lies in explicit knowledge and information. If either side would have the same information and explicit knowledge about the inanimate issues, they would have the same opinion. If the information required to take a decision is completely available to the responsible manager, she will take the required decision and there cannot be any conflict about the decision. Conflict happens in such cases as the two sides have considered different set of facts to arrive at their conclusions. The ensuing discussion or debate offers either side of the conflict and opportunity to gather new pieces of information. A listening attitude borne out of faith, trust, and belief in the purpose improves the amount of relevant explicit knowledge to conclude the best decision. Therefore, this is still a good conflict to have and debates or arguments can be excellent instruments to collect relatively unknown facts from either side of the conflict.

Leadership uses such a good conflict as an envelope of opportunity to develop knowledge and raise the bar. Could lead to innovation, creativity, development of others, and contribute to SPG.

Bad Conflict—A Difference of Purpose

Conflicts become more and more difficult to manage when the purpose of working together becomes ambiguous or controversial. Gradually, people form ghettoes or start pushing their personal purposes. Quickly enough, the ghettoed purposes become stronger drivers than the organization's purpose and results in a complete alienation between two sides. They lose sight of the reason for working together. Once the common purpose, the edifice on which stands the very concept of a group or a team, starts crumbling, human emotions like faith, trust, and belief—the glue that binds people together—go up in smoke. Even self-confidence or convictions take a battering. Each individual gets relegated to animalistic behaviour with defence ramparts being set up in haste and offense ammunition deployed at the slightest of provocation. An acrid smell pervades everything and we have a bad conflict on our hands.

The good conflict turns into bad conflict with the mere perception of a conflict about the purpose to work together.

The root cause for differences between two sides of a conflict lies in *Why* something has to be done and not about the tasks (*Whats*), processes (*Hows*), or resources (*With Whats*). Unless both sides come to an agreement on this Why, it remains a conflict of purpose. Can they any longer be called a team, an organization, or a company? Can they work together?

Yes, they can, provided one side has no option but to accept what the other side demands. We have a predatory situation in full flush. Mildly speaking, management by Theory X combined with guile, deception, trickery, cunningness, and a rule of the powerful comes to roost. You have the compliant side working for fulfilment of their lower level needs while the commanding side has to continuously find ammunition to keep dangling different carrots or sticks of motivation. This approach is quite scientific, embedded in motivational tactics to achieve incremental work produced by people driven by the short term. Such people could well be leaders in their individual lives but never inside that organization, where they are forced to work without agreeing on the purpose. There would be a few managers on the complying side of the conflict that the commanding side would need to fulfil 'their' purpose. The zamindars with their *Munims* and *Lathails*[25] in India did it very well as long as it lasted, and the Manchester mill owners with their gun toting supervisors[26] too succeeded with such leadership or would one call it management culture. But, such complete divide in purpose is rarely found in today's knowledge organizations.

What is more prevalent today is a perception divide in organizational purpose between two sides of a conflict. It looks almost inevitable in knowledge organizations of today that have developed into quite complex structures due to several factors like:

---

[25] *Munims* were the manager cum chief accountants and *Lathails* were the stick wielding bouncers employed by the *Zamindars*

[26] The managers guarded the mill and its surrounding community to ensure that the skilled textile machine operators were not meeting outsiders and getting wooed away by other mill owners

- Functional organizations with increasing depth in knowledge creation as well as management. This has given rise to strong functional KPIs[27] driving efficacy and efficiency through each individual working for that function.
- Project management activities requiring cross functional teams to work together with perceived conflict in functional and project priorities.
- Business processes running across various functions leading to top management being responsible for process KPIs while functional managers are expected to deliver their functional KPIs.
- Complexity of measuring and rewarding individuals for conflicting KPIs.

While the above factors pose real challenges to managers, real life never runs exactly as per planned processes, deadlines, or KPIs. A minor change in context or unforeseen events are enough to force a compromise between the individual, functional, and the process KPIs. This pits team members and functional managers at loggerheads and across perceived divides. The overarching or the enterprise goals are related to the business processes spanning various functions and hence, such conflicts finally land up on the top management plate that is already overflowing with enough complexity from their task of 'transforming Rome'. These are very 'busy' managers, or that's what they believe. They are forced to find time to take the decisions but not to offer explanations to their functional managers, why they decided as they did. In order to balance the enterprise's objectives, their decisions to resolve such conflicts do

[27] Key Performance Indicators

go against one function or project. They expect their managers to simply implement their decisions. This is what creates a bad conflict despite a firm decision being taken to be followed and no personal agenda. Functional or project managers not offered time consuming explanations interpret such decisions as biased in favour of certain managers or projects. This leads to demotivation for those who perceived the decisions to be biased against them. On the other hand, the narcissistic tendencies of those managers who perceived the decision coming out in their favour received a fillip. The result is predatory behaviour, narcissism, grudging work, and drooping shoulders. All this could have been avoided if the top management would have found some additional time to explain to all concerned the constraints and merits of their decision.

Let's look at an illustration. An R&D team was on the verge of a breakthrough with an innovation that would create a longer-term entry barrier for a product line. They needed some critical capital investments to proof their innovation. The product manager from the marketing function was pushing R&D to work on shorter-term cosmetic improvements for the existing products to achieve his KPIs that required the gross profits to be perked up. It was not for the functional managers to decide upon the choice. The top management took up this topic in the next management meeting and decided 'in favour' of the marketing silo. The marketing manager now walked with a swagger while the petulance in the R&D team was palpable when they were refused the capex. The demotivated R&D team could not give it all to the improvement requests from the product manager and the result was no increase in gross profit. The breakthrough innovation got relegated to the next year's budget. At the end of the year, the top management found the overall enterprise objectives sacrificed both for the short term as well as the long term.

Leadership—Explanations to Create a Common Purpose

The conflicts are created by the decisions that hit functional management without the rationale for the same. The line managers too have arguments and counter arguments that remain unaddressed. While, management has to take decisions, they depend on their line managers for the action and results. These line managers may well be 'followers' in the management hierarchy, but are knowledge workers and not Frederick Taylor's pin makers from the 20th century. Unless they understand or buy in into the bias for action, conflict will prevail and push the organizations into the motivation arena. No volitional can act without an attachment to the purpose of action.

> *Explanation of the rationale for decisions taken and creating the acceptance of the common purpose is the supreme task of leadership today.*

Leaders have the power of empathy and therefore understand *why* others may not appreciate what they understand as the reason for the decision taken. Leaders understand that the context handled by those inflicted by their decisions is not the same as what the decision maker considers for taking the decision. Therefore, they take pains to explain to all stakeholders why the decision makes sense for the organization. They specifically plan Time in their calendars and call for meetings with all stakeholders with the sole purpose of explanation. They realize that explanation is one of the primary tasks of leaders. They have learnt that explanation to others' question—Why?—is a great investment that ensures best results from the decisions taken. Even external consultants can take an appropriate decision (advice given) and walk away. One does not need managers or management to merely conclude decisions like consultants. The knowledge worker or a manager irrespective of their position in the decision hierarchy of an organization needs a *bias* for action. Leadership is to provide that *bias* as that in turn creates volitional engagement and future leadership.

Management or managers transform into leaders when they have learnt the significance of explanations, subconsciously or consciously. This usually comes from numerous change management experiences in their lives—whether in the work or personal domain. For example, an individual who gets explanation by his parents as to why they took decisions that they had to and had friends whose parents resorted to just short bursts of instructions would have understand why parents asked their children to do certain things. At times, he explained to his instructed friends why their parents wanted them to do what they were asked to do. When such an individual becomes a manager, he is more likely to knowingly or unknowingly believe in McGregor's Theory Y principles. When forced to take decisions as management to others, he would offer explanations due to his habits of old and successfully prevent an environment of compliance and command and rather encourage debates and explanations that would make his followers more volitionally engaged.

Therefore, leaders develop a habit to invest in explanations at the beginning of the change management process. They learn that investment in the art of explanation generates more leadership resources including time for them to create further value for their organization or life. They know that this pathway saves them from the exhausting task of supervising human resources that are motivationally engaged. In today's knowledge society where people work across large physical distances, from home, across continents, and with dependency on individual competencies, supervision is a waste of time for both the manager and the managed. Fortunately, there are many who have learnt not to follow the management practices of the erstwhile zamindars of India or the gun-toting mill managers of Manchester.

> *Leaders do not have to worry about motivational tactics to manage unwilling humans as they have learnt the power of explanations and the art of creating a common purpose.*

5
The Followers

The entire world of managers and those interested or invested in the domain of management have written volumes on leadership. I too followed suit and wrote some more. But, not many have attempted to write about followers. Is it because 'followership' is considered a lesser challenge than leadership? Or is it because followership does not add as much value as leadership?

Maybe, writers/investigators do not find it as self-levitating as when dabbling in leadership. Or, it could be that followers being too many and leaders too few, it is easier to notice leadership or the absence of it. After all, the expected impact from leadership in enterprise or society at large does appear to be work in progress with a lot to be desired but not delivered. That is why the academics keep churning out book after book on this hackneyed topic and breed.

Followers are lambasted day in and out with the idiosyncrasies of their leaders. They are sometimes treated as the experimental laboratories for the ideas and decisions that their leadership hurls at them without any validation. Emails hit smart phones like lightning and followers cower at these Damocles swords waiting for the thunder in the offing. Responding to them means some kind of commitment and one may not be entirely prepared for it as there are too many already grinding away at your scant resources. Trepidation, perspiration, blood pressure, pills, hospitalization, and even recovery under the glare of waiting emails or projects is what haunts most followers in the business world of so much to get with so little time at hand. Most followers retire night after night dreading the pink slips prowling outside that could blow into smithereens their plastic securities.

Sounds precarious—the life of followers! But, is that the reality?

The followers of today are not the illiterate, innocent lambs of the pre-knowledge society whose survival depended upon the rations or benevolence granted by their chiefs. Their managers (expected to be leaders!) need not be looked upon as mere whip wielding brutes whose only passion is to make the followers keep pulling at their oars in sync with their KPI drumbeats. The followers of today are knowledge bearers on whose capabilities depends the success of their leadership. They are not just doers of biddings handed down. They are the analysts, the creators and implementers of logic, reason, and action leading to results. While the onus of figuring out the future lies on the leadership, the followers figure out the way to drive through each inch of the journey. This journey is no longer about brawn and rowing with heavy oars. This is made possible by the brains and the knowledge of the followers.

Followership is as important as leadership. Followership is also about leaders figuring out the details of each inch of progress. Each follower is a leader in her or his own right crunching the relative complexity of their respective domains, creating entry barriers and competitive advantages around their playground. They are constantly developing not only their own expertise and knowledge, but also tirelessly developing their own followers as each inch of progress depends on the state-of-art of their knowledge and expertise.

Followership is not anymore about waiting for instructions and efficiently completing the task. It is about an incessant search for better ways, smarter results, newer knowledge development, and specialization. Supervision is no longer the way to achieve the results of today. Delivering on your own with 100 percent quality as per plans and commitment without any monitoring by your seniors makes you more valuable and valued to the organization. Supervisory layers of organization are dwindling fast with knowledge management and technology taking over. Each individual in the modern organization is on her own to know what, how, when something has to be done. This releases the manager to similarly contribute with her own knowledge in her own domain or context. A leader-followers' combination where each individual delivers 100 percent as per their roles without the need for any supervision or expectation from each other is more productive for the enterprise than a much larger supervision-oriented team.

Followership is no longer positioned below the leadership level. The combine of leadership and followership better fits the shape of a matrix, where each role complements the other. Gone are the days when you could build a strategy without followership and simply direct them to follow through. Today no strategy is built without the active involvement or contribution from the followership.

> *Gone are the days when followership was about fulfilling the expectations of the leadership. Today followers can create their own trajectories and have a chance to go beyond any expectations.*

6

Redundancy and the Growth Engine

A business enterprise is akin to a human being. It even has its own hierarchy of needs as discussed in Part 3. It starts from an embryonic existence created by the entrepreneurial mating of ideas and desire. The initial years are solely dependent on the entrepreneurial parenting just as the human child is. Thereafter comes a stage when the entrepreneur's energies as well as expertise are not enough to help the enterprise grow anymore.

Redundancy as a phenomenon takes over the organization. The entrepreneurs become redundant and have to be replaced by the managers. The leadership culture of looking 'up' to the entrepreneur gets gradually replaced with looking 'across' at peers and team members for leadership. But, unlike human beings, enterprises have the potential to be perennial. Hence, nothing that runs the enterprise or is run with, can last an enterprise's life span. Something new has to replace the old all the time. It is simple logic—unless something becomes redundant, how can anything new 'grow' up and take its place? We could talk about tools, systems, products, technology, processes, knowledge, people, or even management. All these instruments of an organization are on the winding pathway of growth—a journey from inception to a natural death. Hence, before redundancy is forced upon any of these instruments including managers, working on making ourselves redundant over a period of time would be the way to crank up a new phase of growth for the organization. While leadership culture can act as the fuel, redundancy is what fires up the engine of growth in an organization.

Redundancy goes through the mature stage of *Vanaprastha* to shortly taper off into *Sanyasa*[28] followed by death. All the above organizational instruments develop from relative infancy to grow into powerful utilities only to mature into static, and finally reducing returns for their costs. The non-human instruments get depreciated against their capital costs, while the living instruments like people and management continue to take incremental salaries without producing proportionate value once they reach their maturities. This is the reason that people in organizations are ready enough to accept redundancy of inanimate instruments like tools, systems, technology, processes, etc. But, when it comes to redundancy of issues internalized or embodied in the human form, things start becoming sticky. This happens because most people are motivated to become successful as quickly as possible but do not think about their becoming redundant for their roles in due course of time.

After gaining the ability or knowledge for a certain domain or role, most individuals have an ardent need to celebrate and enjoy their success. This makes them pause mentally. While they relax a bit and bask in their well-deserved short-term success like the fabled hare, the tortoise of knowledge lumbers by rendering them relatively redundant. They could be innocently oblivious of the principle of redundancy—'Whatever got you

---

[28] Vanaprastha and Sanyasa are two of the four stages of a human life as per vedic scriptures. Please see Chapter 1, Part 6

where you are is not enough to keep you there'. Another reason for redundancy being stickier for people is the fear of becoming unwanted. This fear is not misplaced as long as you are a skilled person as opposed to one with accumulated tacit knowledge. I use the word skill to signify explicit knowledge that can be learnt easily by others over a finite period of time. This is normally true for most routine or simple tasks as defined in the Stacey's Matrix, while tacit knowledge would mostly apply to complicated tasks (Parts 1 and 5) gained through practice and experience. Hence, investment in your complicated zones and gaining tacit knowledge could be one way to prevent the threat of redundancy.

However, redundancy like many things in real life offers a sunnier side too. While the downside of the redundancy principle is the gradually reducing returns on your costs to the organisation, the upside is that of growth. To enjoy the sunnier side you should not *become* redundant; you need to *make* yourself redundant for the role you are in while simultaneously building yourself up for the next levels of complexity or in simpler terms, for levels that are of higher value in the organization. One becomes redundant when we take a knowledge break and do not continue to develop ourselves.

Let us look at an illustration. A frontline sales person was promoted as the manager for his team. As the manager, he became quite successful in running his small team of sales and service specialists and delivered satisfactory results for three years in a row. He did his team leader's job well and his team too developed into strong independent performers. But, he was on a knowledge break as he stopped developing himself for the next possible levels of responsibility. When a position opened up for the next level, he was not considered as he did not have the required grasp in financial statements, strategy development, working with senior management, etc. In another few years, the top management had to cut costs of redundancy and our good sales manager on a knowledge break found himself replaced by one of his star performers.

Instead, you can *make* yourself redundant by first developing with the context you need to manage in and then developing others to take over what you become good at. Secondly, you need to study and learn on your own about the contexts managed by your seniors or any other positions that you would like to grow up into. Once you make yourself redundant for the role you are in and are relatively conversant with the context to be managed for higher or other exciting responsibility positions, you are ready for greater challenges in the same organization or another. Luckily, the knowledge society or organization we live in today offers roles that are not static in its knowledge needs. Change as the consistent partner of knowledge society has been forcing redundancy of knowledge faster and faster. Redundancy of knowledge offers managerial roles a continuous growth opportunity. Once you master the potential of growth for the role you are in, you can announce yourself redundant and be on offer to the same organization or another for roles with better returns to the organization and consequently for yourself.

Organizations that are in the business of growth are perennially suffering from a paucity of such growth creating knowledge workers (leaders). It is a rare breed yet, that has the hunger for new knowledge and capabilities that finds them new perches on the growth ladder of an organization. In time, it is this hunger that infects them with the self-confidence of investing into their zones of complexity and announcing their redundancy. By doing so, they are recognized for adding additional value to their organizations and consequently to themselves by default.

But, before you think of making yourself redundant, you need to go through the four stages of the learning cycle in your role. It is a journey from relative (1) Unconscious Inability to (2) Conscious Inability to (3) Conscious Ability to (4) Unconscious Ability as shown in Fig. 13 in relation to time and value for the organization as well as the individual.

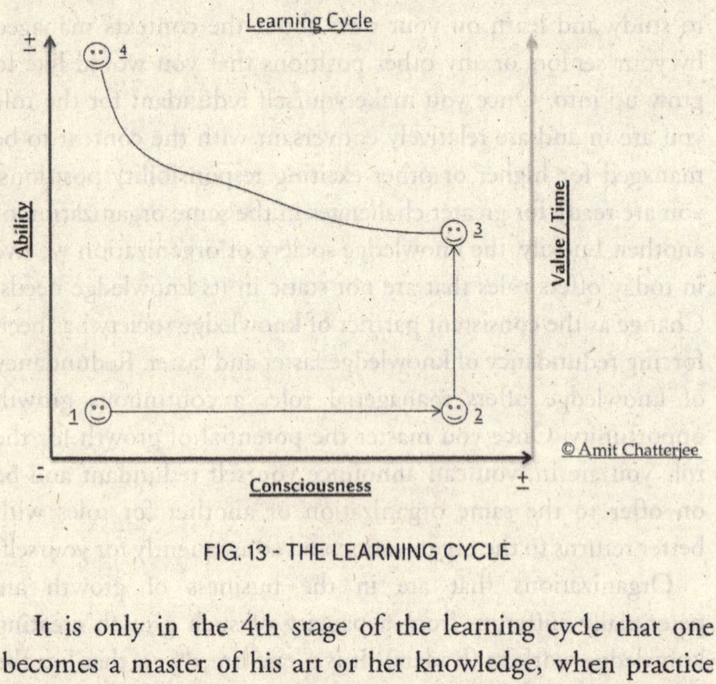

FIG. 13 - THE LEARNING CYCLE

It is only in the 4th stage of the learning cycle that one becomes a master of his art or her knowledge, when practice (numerous applications to real life) of the knowledge makes you embrace the varying angularities of each situation while in stride. The 4th stage of unconscious ability is where the knowledgeable person is able to adapt his knowledge to fit or fix the context.

A fitting analogy lies in driving a car: the 3rd phase is when you have learnt to drive a car but you are nervous when your phone rings. The 4th phase is when your mind is going through the meeting you have to run to in an hours' time, while you decide to change your route looking at the navigation and then dial your spouse to call the plumber to look at the kitchen sink.

That is when you are running your role or job with your gaze hooked by the vision or purpose of your role and not completing a difficult task to perfection. That is when you are able to think of the future and think of the person in your team who could succeed you in your role. That is when you have the time and sense of purpose to groom your successor. That is when you have the time and are able to sense what new knowledge or challenge you could dive into in your organization for taking up new and bigger responsibilities for yourself. You are now worth your weight in knowledge and ready for your redundancy. Once you are ready, you are noticed by your management to take over bigger roles where someone else has become or made himself redundant. It is a cyclic or a crankshaft action. One redundancy feeds into the other up the value or knowledge chain. *That is what I call the Growth Engine.*

It was not so long back when redundancy and negative returns on costs coincided with a man's working lifespan. Companies took pride and found peace in offering lifetime employment. The knowledge society of today is changing this quite rapidly. Lifetime employment was possible as long as enterprises had no real competition or found competitive advantage as technology or cost leaders. With growing competition due to globalization and widespread availability of knowledge workers, employees have to either keep upgrading their knowledge in the same roles or acquire new knowledge to become potentials for new or bigger roles. Even low paid roles in developing economies are not getting spared from redundancy as technology and systems invade suddenly but surely to replace manual simple tasks. As knowledge becomes redundant at ever increasing speed, people as carriers of such knowledge run the risk of becoming redundant unless they 'upgrade' their knowledge in line with the changing contexts—markets, customers, competition, substitution, speed, perceived quality, or just the quality of commitments required. It is for the naive to be surprised by redundancy.

The knowledge worker today is on a fast train towards redundancy.

However, for those who are raring to fill up these redundancies at higher returns on costs, this is good news, this is growth. As they step into new domains of relative complexity for themselves and enjoy the challenge of using their knowledge and growing with it, life is great. Celebrations, consumerism, narcissistic satisfactions become the normal and possibly deserved indulgencies. But beware, as you too may end up being redundant if you do not go for the next 'upgrade' in line with the changing contexts.

Hence, redundancy is the spark that cranks up growth; redundancy of one brings in the other who is motivated and ready to stoke the fire. But, the spark needs appropriate fuel to keep the fire burning and creating further growth for the organization. This fuel comes from the leadership culture in the organization that makes people sense the disruptive opportunities in their environment. (I use the word disruption here more as a change from within rather than from outside.) A leadership culture that nurtures volitional engagement makes it possible for those at near redundancy levels or at the peak of their Learning Cycle to grab the disruption opportunities. Such a culture supported by the management of the enterprise celebrates the snowballing of such initiatives into movements of change resulting in growth for the organization and such leader managers.

Such disruptions are necessary as an organization is largely a 'limited' entity tending to settle down with status quos. It is limited by the running business, the market, the customers, technology, management style, functions, and by finance. These limits remain quite rigid until disruption of some form hits the organization. Changes in the limited contexts can create differentiation between one organization and its possible competition. This differentiation gives rise to competitive advantage or entry barriers that would form the cornerstones for sustained profitable growth of the organization.

PART 5

The Synthesis

This part is not a gist of all that precedes it or what keeps humming in the mind of the author. It is rather written with a focus on the purpose of Growth Management, with the onus solely on the leader manager.

- *'Evolution of a Leader' traces the journey of an individual from its parenting edifice and anoints the manager with the great opportunity of developing leadership potential. It culminates in explaining the characteristics of a leader as it evolves into an individual with distinction.*
- *'Growth Management' seeks to seal the definition of a Leader Manager as being solely responsible for managing growth. While it can be the author's dilemma, if that is possible for all readers or not, the reader is left with no comfort to be a Growth Manager and not accept being a Leader.*

1

Evolution of a Leader

'We have been so burdened with duties that we have never learnt the delights of responsibility, of making a difference to somebody or something... Not everyone can handle the same amount of space and responsibility... Too much space can cause an error or an accident. Too little, can impoverish a life.'

CHARLES HANDY[29]

Just like an idea is born in the mind of a person steered by experiences and a combination of the subconscious and pursued purpose of existence, a leader too is born of its parents and influenced by their upbringing and the life they lead. The idea or the child continues to evolve with influences from other family members too and later from outsiders. The child develops his foundation mainly under the influence of parenting. With increasing exposures from outside the family, the child finally blooms into adolescence and starts developing a personality and mind of his own. Next, he goes on to hit the world of work and is known by a name that embodies the habits of thinking and action the young individual grew up with. This is when

[29] Handy, C., (1994), *The Empty Raincoat*, First published by Hutchison, reprinted by Random House UK Ltd., London

the pressures of the workplace, the profession, the professional knowledge, and the culture of the organization as influenced by its management embraces the individual for the better part of his waking hours. Under the deliberate or default influence of the manager starts the *construction* phase of the individual's evolution. The personality and the germs of leadership as scripted during the foundation phase now gets sculpted or stunted under the influence of the manager, the entrusted representative of the management of the organization. The manager not only plays a very important role in the quality of construction of the mind and personality, but more significantly remains responsible for the *foundation* she selected or rejected for their workplace. With passage of time, the personality and the mind keeps evolving, influenced by varied experiences and finally matures into the individual we all become. It is like the *soul* of a building whose *foundation* was laid by its parents and the *construction* influenced by its manager(s).

The soul of the individual under the above formative influences develops a sense of appreciation for values, principles, habits, behaviour, choices—the entire grounding for an approach to life. It develops a taste for science, art, social issues, or just remains non-committal.

> *From an innocent idea, the child evolves into a full blown individual personality of an adult man or woman, distinctly different from all others around.*

He may become an expert in some domain or a generalist with multi-tasking skills. He may become a voluble extrovert or a studious introvert. He may be motivated by short-term motivators or have the mindset to hook onto larger or distant purposes. He may be a deceptive narcissist or spread development through constructive narcissism. He may be content with little or develop the intensity of relentless pursuit of self-esteem crutches. He may evolve into the ever-curious hunter of new knowledge, unsatiated by what he knows or become the passionate executor of correctness purely driven by the beauty of perfection. He may manifest the ghosts of irresponsible parenting as a reactive narcissist or be disillusioned early with inanimate or material challenges to immerse himself into social development. He may remain perennially occupied trying to fulfil other's expectations or choose to lead a life beyond expectations.

Whichever way the individual evolves, the trajectory will be determined largely by the sculpting undergone during the initial years of managerial enculturation, while the psychological basis can usually be traced back to the edifice built under parental influence.

The soul of the individual gets developed by the habits of thinking and action, the principles of reverence and exclusion and the sense of right and wrong that are embedded in the foundation and the influences during personality construction. The individual who learns to make choices, swims in waters of complexity, holds on to values that stand the test of the long term, casts his visionary ropes across the canyon of risks, and develops others as conscientious leaders would be the one who evolves as a leader. This leader will always catalyse remarkable achievements and contribute to a society that is happy, creative, and worth living for.

The Foundation Phase

The parents transfer the genes and more importantly influence the habits of thinking and action of their children by the way *they* live their own lives. Parents are also riding the trajectory of their own formative and experiential lives. They have developed habits they unknowingly practice and adhere to behaviour and values they grew up with. The child learns from observation and is encultured by the environment he grows up in. In the initial phase, he absorbs the influences unknowingly from his parents and other family members. As the child toddles out into the outside world of influences, the initial imprints from his parents makes it react in a certain manner when faced with unfamiliar situations. He is shy or friendly, inquisitive or accepting, compliant or opinionated, patient or aggressive. He becomes withdrawn or enthusiastic, demonstrative or subdued, all because of parental influence. However, the fact remains that most parents nurture their children without any objective of developing their leadership mindset. They give them love, affection, care, meet their needs out of emotions, habits, and a sense of duty. There is no such thing as a 'professional parent' with any professional knowledge of parenting or an objective of developing children as leaders.

Just like a new manager, the parents slide into their roles without any formal training in parenting a child. Parents probably are more confused about the final results they have to deliver than managers are in their new positions. Of course, a lot among the urban educated read books on how to rear a child. This can be compared to spending one or two years in a business school with the expectation of learning management. If learning how to rear a child is the same as knowing how to be a good parent, then all MBAs would have been elegantly facile in practising leadership. Organizations would have been bursting at their seams with creativity, innovation, greatness, and development of conscientious leaders. And Dr Benjamin Spock would have been enough to create a civilized society.

I have no intention to pontificate on what may constitute good parenting (I am on my own journey as a practising parent). My effort lies in sensitizing my readers to their responsibility as well as potential to influence good leadership values and trajectories as managers and parents as and when applicable.

The Construction Phase

The responsibility to recruit a knowledge worker opens up the door for a manager to develop leadership mettle for the future. The moment the manager interviews an individual, she has the chance to assess the foundation and exercise her option to select or reject the same. She has a good chance to succeed in developing conscientious managers in the future, if she is careful to use her knowledge of managerial science. Once the foundation is selected with care, the possibility of a manager or management to sculpt and not stunt the leadership potential of an individual should be easier than parenting. After all, the manager unlike a parent is quite clear about the results she has to deliver and that too as milestones over a foreseeable period of time. No knowledge worker is selected to deliver the results of the short term. A manager can plan the development trajectory possible for the recruit over some years and coach the individual's development accordingly. The manager can look upon herself as the Designer of the Individual's Role and allow him appropriate freedom to explore his leadership potential.

I offer two constructs that could be very useful for managers to sculpt the leadership potential of individuals for whom they are responsible.

Construct 1—Handy's Doughnut Principle

The construct is about giving the individual a choice, a real choice. Charles Handy used an inside-out doughnut where there is space around the core inside. He talked about two levels of accountability for an individual, be it a manager or her employee. Type I is about the 'Duties' that constitute the job and the results required from the role that the individual has to perform. Type I accountability is mandatory and the core of the doughnut (Fig. 14).

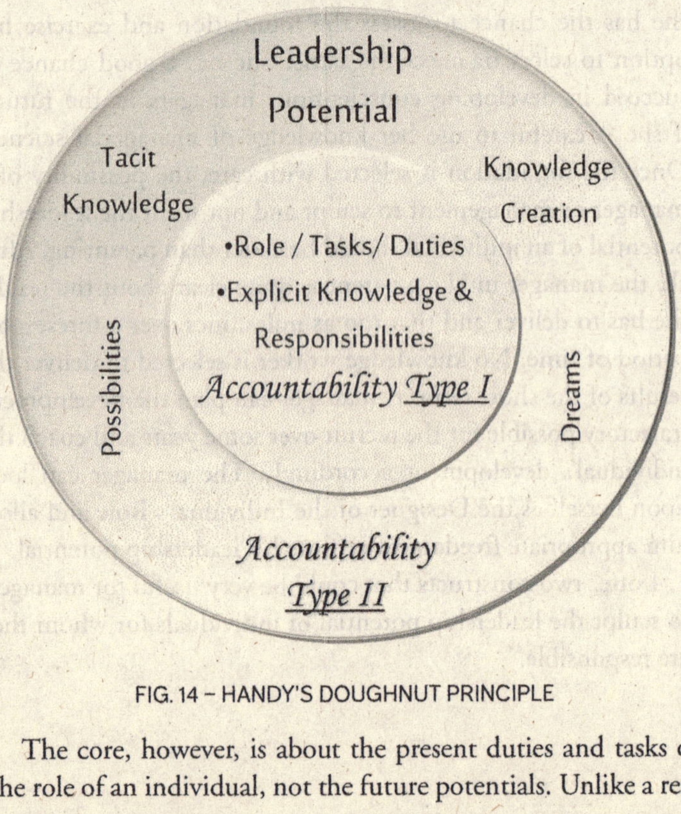

FIG. 14 – HANDY'S DOUGHNUT PRINCIPLE

The core, however, is about the present duties and tasks of the role of an individual, not the future potentials. Unlike a real machine or a Taylorian one (an expert in one singular skill), the knowledge worker or an individual is not a Capex investment churning out the same results year after year till breakdown and replacement. The individual will and can develop greater knowledge and varied taste in time and could take up roles with different or higher value contribution in the future. Even the current role can be expanded in its reach and value once the individual develops further. Type II accountability leads to tapping the leadership potential of the individual in the present and inspires the doughnut manager to allow the shaded space beyond Type I for the individual to discover his potential beyond the explicit knowledge domain of Type I accountability.

Each one of us has more potential than what is utilized by our Type I roles. Herein lays the scope to learn the art of envisioning, developing ones tacit knowledge, and unleashing its development potential. Managers in the business of developing leadership have a radar sense that catches and instigates such development tendencies. They help the individual to develop competencies outside their current explicit domains. Handy explained, 'It is no longer about the manager and the managed, but the designer of the doughnut and the occupant—a relationship built more on trust and mutual respect than on control.' Let us look at the two cases below.

Case I—A manager I know had a very competent assistant working for him for several years. She was competent in her role and smart enough to handle many diverse issues. He used to sometimes share some HR topics with her although that was not part of her explicit role. He observed that she had an interest in such issues. One day he asked her what she would do if he were to leave the company. She was initially shocked thinking her manager was planning to leave the company. The question also raised her anxiety levels as she had never thought of such a predicament. The manager explained that he was not planning any such move but it was an eventuality he wanted her to think about. After a few days, she came up with a wish to do an MBA in HR while on the job. The manager gladly agreed to support her. In few years' time, when the company needed to expand its HR team, the lady was selected for the position and now works as an *Assistant Manager*—HR in the same company.

The assistant had the foundation—the manager was on the watch for developing his people, volitionally—the discussions, and instigation to explore beyond her Type I role sculpted the assistant's mind to think beyond her explicit role—the leadership mind of the assistant made her choose and invest in her own development. The foundation and the construction support developed the assistant for the future. She was not offered any motivational carrot or stick and was offered the freedom to choose on her own. Later, the company needed a manager or leader and it was available in-house—the company gained and so did the individual. The manager did not have any unfulfilled needs to fulfil for doing what he did as a habit; he was a leader in action who tapped the leadership potential of his employee.

Case II—In a company, the tea/coffee machine was unlocked three times a day during stipulated coffee and lunch breaks. All engineers would flock and queue up for their cuppa. The underlying idea was to control costs and indiscipline—the manager did not want people going for coffee other than at official breaks as that might increase the costs and make work suffer. The coffee breaks were respite from work. Due to changes in the business context, the manager got changed!

The new manager came from a different foundational upbringing. He decided to keep the coffee machine open at all times and announced that people could have coffee at will;

however they should be personally responsible for their work commitments. Engineers (knowledge workers) now went up to the canteen for their cuppa whenever they really felt like having one. They did not have to wait for breaks. They knew that they could have a coffee whenever they wanted to and in effect, quite a few never went more than once as they were engaged in their work without being constrained by rules. Most people went in working groups to discuss problems over coffee. Earlier, they would only go to the manager with their problem when they were reviewed in a daily meeting. The decisions from the manager would be followed but with constant rumblings of bad conflicts. The new manager had stopped the daily review meetings and instead had asked team leaders to go for a celebration with their teams when they finished a project before time. Of course, monthly review meetings were mandatory, but for team leaders to share their achieved milestones and planned successes. Problems were now largely solved by the teams themselves and seldom reached the manager. The manager normally had to get involved to facilitate change management, unravel good conflicts and administrative decisions.

The leadership culture now believed in individuals being responsible and civilized enough to understand their priorities of life (with work as a subset). This manager believed that knowledgeable adults need not be controlled and should be allowed more space to design and decide their own work and fun. Coffee consumption went down by 20 percent, work improved by miles. No supervision was required. The team was volitionally engaged. There was no requirement for motivational carrots or sticks.

Space means freedom but it increases complexity. Complexity is where leadership rears its head and thrives. Not allowing space means that the full possibilities of the situation have not been exploited or developed. An individual feels responsible only when he can make choices and there is a risk of making errors. Allowing space to individuals breeds responsibility.

Thankfully, there is space beyond the Type I core of duty to live up to our full potential—*bildung (self development)*—and be on a journey towards *aham brahma (In me, I can find the supreme).*

Construct 2—Breaching the Motivation–Volition Barrier

For every individual there lies a motivation–volition barrier. This is the Rubicon one needs to cross to become volitionally engaged. As explained in the sections on Motivation and Volition Arena in Part 3, leadership is only possible through volitional engagement. While the onus of crossing the Rubicon lies on the individual, a manager can act as a facilitator through discussions or debates or by assigning tasks that help the individual transcend into a *post-decisional implementation state* or into the volitional arena. Remember, the *pre-decisional mentation* state of mind is the motivation arena. Once, we are in the volitional arena, the leadership mind is hooked by the purpose and ceases to dither about gains or pains.

In practice, the same barrier can be seen better using the Stacey's Matrix as shown again in Fig. 15. Managers can help in the construction of the leader by assigning a mix of tasks that has some complex tasks for the individual. The manager needs to bear in mind that the tasks assigned should be complex for the leader under development, not necessarily for others. In the zone of complexity lies the scope for 'remarkable achievements' and manifestation of leadership thinking and activity—being creative, innovative, attaining greatness, developing, exploring and choosing from conjured options, decision making, and sustained implementation of a choice. Let us discuss these task types and see where the motivation–volition barrier lies.

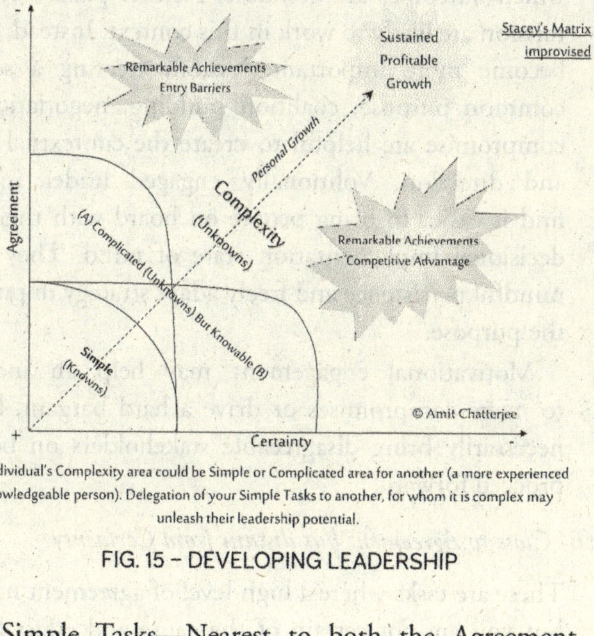

Every Individual's Complexity area could be Simple or Complicated area for another (a more experienced or knowledgeable person). Delegation of your Simple Tasks to another, for whom it is complex may unleash their leadership potential.

FIG. 15 – DEVELOPING LEADERSHIP

- Simple Tasks—Nearest to both the Agreement and Certainty

  For simple tasks, one can use past experience to predict the future. One can plan specific pathways of action to achieve outcomes and monitor actual results by comparing it against these plans. The goal is to repeat what is known to work and motivational engagements could be useful to improve efficiency and effectiveness. Most day-to-day operational tasks in an organization belong to this category.

- Complicated Tasks

(A) Close to Certainty but distant from Agreement

Some issues have a great deal of certainty about how outcomes are created but lack of agreement about which outcomes are desirable. Neither plans nor shared mission are likely to work in this context. Instead, politics become more important. Vision, creating a sense of common purpose, coalition building, negotiation, and compromise are helpful to create the contextual agenda and direction. Volitionally engaged leader managers find it easier to bring people on board with their post–decisional implementation state of mind. They pursue mindful persistence and freely adapt strategy in pursuit of the purpose.

Motivational engagement may help an individual to make compromises or drive a hard bargain, but not necessarily bring disagreeable stakeholders on board to proceed forward.

(B) Close to Agreement but distant from Certainty

These are tasks where a high level of agreement may exist but you are not certain of the cause and effect linkages to create desired outcomes. Monitoring against a pre-set plan will obviously not work. Instead, a strong sense of shared mission and vision may go a long way. In such contexts, the way forward is to head towards an agreed upon future state even though the specific pathways cannot be predetermined. As past habits would not be of much help, hurdles and errors would be natural and the resilience needed to overcome them can come only from volitional energy.

Motivational engagement does not work here either as there would be no security for gratification of unfulfilled needs for the individual. Higher the hurdles or challenges, faster their hopes evaporate and earlier they jump ship.

- Complex Tasks–The Zone of Complexity

  The zone of complexity is filled with complete uncertainty and lack of agreement between stakeholders. This is the temple of leadership development as traditional management approach or habits of knowns do not apply anymore.

  The purpose is to fructify the vision that the individual is hooked with. A step into one's zone of complexity is like feeling the chill of the water on a cool evening. It sends a current up your spine only to steel up the resolve, the will that makes one cross the Rubicon. The individual is severed in this zone from the past and discovers ways to reach the larger objective or withdraws, accepting defeat. This is where the individual's foundation is tested. If the management had selected the right foundation, you will see the leader emerging. The right foundation would trigger creativity and innovation in this zone and contribute to entry barriers and competitive advantages for the organization.

  Motivational engagement is of no use in your zone of complexity. Volitional pursuit of the vision in a post-decisional implementation state is the only way an individual can lead the way out of complexity.

Managers or management may use this construct based on 'Breaching the Motivation–Volition Barrier' in designing roles, responsibilities, and projects for a planned development of leadership potential. Managers can create an 80:20 or at least a 90:10 mix of tasks with the smaller part being deliberately designed tasks in the zone of complexity for the individual under development. This has become even more significant in today's matriced organizational structures spread across large distances, where the theoretical essence of such structures depends on a pre-determined workflow. This in turn is dependent upon 'simple tasks' and collective responsibility. The real world as always is not made of such innocence, particularly in managerial roles. When complexity due to change in context, conflicts, or unknowns hits such structures, the required rigidity that holds a matriced structure in place prohibits individual initiative, risk, or volitional pursuits. Habits of thinking and action formed under such structures and expectations prevent managers from tackling challenges that require leadership approach. This is probably one of the major reasons for the lament we hear in such organizations about atrophying creativity or innovation.

The Distinct Individual

The foundation was laid over years of parental influence; the managerial masons have done their bit in helping with the construction. In fact, there have been many a mason and artist who left his or her influence on you or me. I was inspired to work with my manager not just because of the vision he articulated but also because of what I had from my foundation. The trajectory of my habits of thinking and action found alignment with what my manager wanted me to get involved in. Later, the reactions between the two forces probably made me make choices that may not have happened if I had not been subjected to these two different influences over different phases of my life. Everything our eyes see, our senses feel or our actions impinge upon, reacts with the residuals in our mind and influences our thoughts unknowingly and continuously. All of us go through such myriad experiences and our minds carry the essence of all those terabytes or petabytes till our last breath. And, all along our journey of life, each decision or choice we make is influenced by the bytes we have assimilated in our minds till that moment. We make errors as well as the best of choices due to the petabytes of our experiences till then. When I do repent a bad habit, the wishful thought that I could go back in time to change it always crosses my mind. My repentance comes from the bytes that I have accumulated till today. The mind that accepted the influence I repent about today was a different mind.

Since, each one of us never has the same set of experiences in our lives, we become distinct from each other. But, that is like every log floating in a river being distinct from the other. Are we supposed to be just a lonely log floating in the river of experiences controlled by our parenting and external influences?

Is our mind only supposed to be a reservoir of retained influences? Doesn't it have any energy to ever decide or make a choice on its own? Will the log of an individual only be battered by what the white water of life subjects it to?

Surely not? Our mind has its own source of energy. Freud said that we have only one source of energy and that is the volitional energy. When we are engaged in something that we like to do, we gain this energy, while it depletes when we are forced to do something that we dislike. Ayn Rand said, 'Free will is the choice to utilize or not utilize one's conceptual faculty. The key to human nature is the fact that man is a being of volitional consciousness...the function of your stomach, lungs, or heart are automatic; that of the mind is not. In any hour or issue of your life, you are free to think or to evade that effort.'[30]

---

[30] Rand, A., (1957), *Atlas Shrugged*, New York; New American Library

Once we decide what we choose to be or to do, we can become a motorized raft in the white water. Our mind becomes then the motor of our life. Surely, it will be buffeted by all the forces that the white water may hurl at us. Stronger the resolve of our minds, better we can survive the temptations, the risks, the waves of onslaughts from the white water of life. But, we also need to have a sense of direction as a rudder for the motorized raft. We need to have an idea about what state of things we wish to be in or where do we want to reach as a vision for ourselves,

FIG. 16 – LIFE IN THE WHITE WATER

for our very own life. This sense of direction would act as the rudder for the motorized raft.

Like any vision, it would be hazy to start with. Yet, we cannot just keep fighting the ferocity of the white water without knowing why we have to fight or where we want to reach.

Like any vision, even the biological one, our vision will gradually sharpen only if we try hard to see, to seek our destination. If we just keep fighting the white water, we will be blinded by the short-term objectives of survival or the delights of a victory. Even if we do survive these skirmishes, such victories would be quite short lived as the forces of the white water are endless. They will keep coming at us in waves, in deceit, or in pricks. The white water of life tends to test not our power of survival but our tenacity to reach our destination. It looks at us in disdain if we do not express our sense of direction and either tries to obliterate us in impatience or simply ignore us for our ignobility. The white water of life is like a powerful intellectual narcissist. It puts you in a spin if you are short sighted, respects you if you measure up to its intensity, or simply discards you as insignificant.

The motor of individuality is our mind. Stronger it is in its resolve, the more respected it is by external influencers. The strength comes from our own mission statement, our sense of values, ethics, and hygiene factors. The sense of direction comes from our very own vision statement. This comes from our sense of purpose, our ownership of long-term objectives for the organization, and our own lives. The white water of life and its forces are not always stronger than our belief in our mission or vision. Leadership is able to wade through uncertainty and weather opposition driven by the power of its mission and vision statements. Actions motivated by crutches offered by organizations or society to shore up our self esteem but not aligned to our values or sense of ethics leads to errors of life. Such a state of mind cannot have the power to prepare for the unforeseen or unexpected that characterizes the complexity domain of leadership.

Complexity is where your 'wanting' to do something stands on quicksand. Motivational temptations cannot go beyond the wanting as the certainty of securing any of the motivators look so bleak. This is where your vision and mission imparts the uncanny senses that hold you on course. The resulting sense of purpose makes you notice several, if not unlimited, options. You have to first 'choose' among those options blinking at you. The only thing that burns bright is the purpose and you know that the fulfilment of the purpose lies beyond the available options. It is your emotional attachment to the purpose that keeps you from discarding it and seeking fulfilment of motivators elsewhere. Your emotions are driven by your value system borne out of your upbringing, sculpted by your experiences over years since your childhood. This is where your formative years steer your approach to the context in a sub-conscious manner and finally catapults you across your Rubicon to a volitional pursuit of the purpose. You make a choice driven by the purpose and not by any motivator.

That is when the individuality of the individual takes form and identity, known for its choices, sense of purpose, and the tenacity to attain it. No longer is he another log floating in the river of life. The individual becomes known for the choices he makes, the opinions, the values, the beliefs he manifests through his decisions and actions. He is known for his sense of direction and therefrom devises a sense of direction for the organization too. The individual becomes the wind and the weathercocks abide by its wishes. The individual becomes the leader as its soul develops through self-knowledge exercising its choices and becomes known for its consistency of character and pursuits.

2
Growth Management

What is a manager's life all about?

They said it is to plan, organize, coordinate, and control the results. I culled the Manager's Maxim (Part 3) from Peter Drucker's five tasks as, 'The Manager sets goals, decides and selects people to accomplish the tasks. He motivates and communicates to integrate people, while being responsible for their development'.

What tasks does the manager's maxim have to accomplish? Is it a one-time task like quarterly or annual results? Once achieved, the manager can retire for the rest of his life? Every manager needs to work for his entire working life. All these periodic results are supposed to coalesce into what? A Manager is not always the CEO of a company. There are scores if not hundreds of managers in an enterprise or organization of a reasonable size. Are they supposed to only 'plan, organize, coordinate, and control' results of the day, the week, the quarter, or the year and be blind about why all that needs to be done?* Is a manager's life simply about earning a monthly cheque and manage his daily, weekly, or annual rations and living costs?

More often than not, the top management is oblivious to this question that needs to be answered in the minds of every manager in an organization. The big chiefs are busy crunching complexity at their stratospheric levels and, like innocent parents, wonder why their managers are not being creative, innovative or leading the way to the future. And trust me, the top management is not going to wake up overnight and devote their time to come and energize you to think beyond the short term. They are mostly too busy and yes, they are also managers and equally short-term oriented for similar reasons. Those few who believe that managers across the length and breadth of their enterprise are potential leaders run the best enterprises in the industry with creativity, innovation, greatness, sustainability, and growth oozing at every nook and corner of their organizations.

This book is not for the top management only, but for any manager at any level or domain in an organization. If you as a manager wish to be in relative control of your future, I encourage you to find your own answers to the above question* and pronto.

It is a no-brainer, really. The manager, like any other human being, needs to grow his income to meet his growing needs and costs. But, the one thing that differentiates a manager from any other professional is that he is managing the business of an enterprise. Be it a team, a division, or an entire company, the enterprise is not headed towards death. Unlike an individual's life, an enterprise's life is perennial and it is the managers of that enterprise who make that possible, not the shareholders. The shareholder is like the jungle man who can bring home some catch (capital) and hopefully some wisdom. The manager on the other hand is the one who cooks the catch, prepares a delicious and healthy plate for all, including the shareholder, to survive and prosper. The manager is the knowledge resource who thinks about how to secure the future of the enterprise.

He uses current resources judiciously and creates resources for the future.

The manager's role is to build people, processes, and knowledge for the coming years and not merely execute the task of the day, month, or the year in an efficient and correct manner. The manager also hunts out markets and upcoming technologies, envisages the future needs for sustained survival, and makes himself increasingly knowledgeable with every passing day or year. The manager feels responsible for his own development and the development of the enterprise's resources.

That is a manager's life. A life devoted to Growth Management.

The manager who is in the business of managing growth for an enterprise is a leader, always on the lookout for remarkable achievements in his or her zones of complexity. Hooked by the purpose of contributing to sustainability, he does everything possible and grows and keeps growing.

Growth management comes only out of individual initiative from the leader manager, not from any named group of managers like the management team (while the named managers can also be leaders). He influences everything in the context he manages including the management of the enterprise. But, the manager also leads a life to fulfil his needs, wants, aspirations, and dreams as work is only a subset of his life. Hence, one needs to be cognizant of the manager's perspective at work as an exercise in alignment with the overall purpose of his life. I present in the graphic below my perspective for a manager's life:

The Imperatives of a Manager's Life

- A manager is a knowledge worker. But, his knowledge is deemed enough only for having reached the current

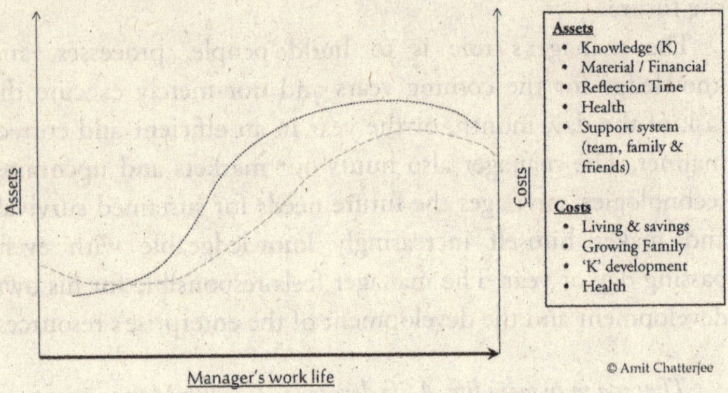

FIG. 17 – A MANAGER'S LIFE AND GROWTH

responsibility position. It is not enough to even continue in the same position for long as the business context keeps changing and others available at lower costs are knocking on management's door for a foothold. A manager has to be ever paranoid about the relevance of his knowledge and be aware of the ever changing horizons. Such a sense does not come from merely being motivationally engaged to tasks or the job.

➢ A manager has to create financial and material assets to provide for the costs and investments in life. The assets are simply required to perform duties, and provide for future needs, comfort, and enjoyment. Having fun is an important need of man as this creates volitional energy. If such assets boost the self esteem of the manager, that can be only a by-product and helps in releasing the person from pursuing short-term self-esteem crutches.

- A manager needs time for reflection. Without creating time, we cannot consciously learn from our past experiences or think of scanning the horizons looking for options to create sustainability, Motivationally engaged managers are focused on their 'expectations being gratified'. They are too busy with the daily grind, keeping a constant tally of the pros and cons, to pause and find time for reflection. The volitionals are ever hunting for options to fructify the post-implementation state.
- A manager has to remain healthy to think, choose, act, and deliver results over a period of time. The temptations of the current are low hanging fruit and enjoyment of the same is the natural tendency of the motivationally engaged!
- A manager needs a support system to lean back on and rejuvenate. We must remember that volitional energy is the only source of energy for the mind of man. Depletion of the volitional energy is natural in a manager's life as you cannot have the luxury of only doing things you like. Relationships based on trust, respect, and transparency with his team members, family, and friends is where a manager can plug in to rejuvenate and recreate himself. The motivationally engaged are in a hurry to gratify their short-term needs. They fail to recognize the need to plan time for recreation or rejuvenation. As a result they normally end up short of relationships based on trust, respect, and transparency.

The above imperatives of a manager's life explain the importance of consistent investment in building assets over the long term to meet the continuous costs of a manager's life. The irony lies in most people losing sight of this obvious long-term perspective. The causation comes from managers managed or driven through motivational engagement that obscures the long term and binds the entire cognizance of a manager on the short term.

Leader managers are better oriented with the long term as their vision and purpose binds them with what has to be made possible over time. They volitionally take on the responsibility of growth management fuelled by their foundation and habits nurtured during their enculturation under proper leadership management. They get hooked by the potential of creating remarkable achievements in their relative complexities. This leads to sustainability of the enterprise and growth for the manager and aligns with the imperatives of a manager's life.

Neither management nor globalization is a trend that may phase out; rather it is a necessity for enterprises worldwide. Enterprises are faced with swathes of change and need for creativity and innovation. This is the universal challenge for all organizations today, be it small, global, profit-oriented, or for social development. Growth management is the need for all enterprises as well as managers. The Practising Manager's Growth Mantra can be used by any manager at any management level, provided the manager makes the choice to be a leader. When practised and nurtured by the top management, it would only get institutionalized and become part of the leadership culture of the organization. Managements have the choice to continue with motivational short-term engagements or utilize individual initiative in relative complexities, catalyse remarkable achievements, and pave the way for sustained profitable growth.

I would like to wrap up with three important contextual challenges that may cast their shadows over growth management prospects or potential of a Leader Manager:

1. Managing the Specialism vs Strategic Paradox

Globalization, competition, speed of change, and sustainability needs have led to a surfeit of diversity and knowledge. All these excesses have swamped managements if not stumped them and forced an acceptance of the paradox of managing specialism and the strategic. Specialism deals with the depth of knowledge and resources required to be developed, maintained and used in functional silos, whereas the strategic deals with the overall objectives of the enterprise. The strategic cannot be achieved by the knowledge silos doing their jobs only. Processes across the functions and decisions taken by the top management influence the outcome of the overall objectives. Domains of specialism are mutating and multiplying every year, be it in product or production technology, processes for customer satisfaction or R&D, HR systems or IT systems, communication tools, machines for data warehousing, analysing and carving niche markets, trade and tariff barriers, international laws and IPR, KPIs and numbers reporting or controlling; the list goes on and on. Managements of small or large enterprises face more and more similar specialist demands and that too with urgency written all across. These specialist demands are critical for short-term survival and naturally hold the eyeballs of the top management.

Managements in the western world as well as academics came up with the much practiced and maligned functional and matrix structures. The functional structures did answer the need for specialism and efficiency. Under proper leadership, it did succeed in creativity, innovation, and development, but were limited to the narrow alleys of one function. Matrix structures evolved over the last few decades to counter the limitations of functional structures. Ironically, what suffers is the strategic or the larger picture management. The larger picture is what constitutes the enterprise's vision, mission, or sustainability objectives leading to growth. In the short term, the larger picture or strategic is also about what the enterprise delivers across the entire business process. The business process is a result of the matriced contribution from the specialist or functional silos. While functional structures gave rise to silo working and mindset, the matrix structures or enterprise objectives were not enough to matrix the minds of the functional contributors. Use of motivation theory linked to incentives for the functional contributors yielded *satisfactory underperformance* as the individuals were motivated in daily lives by their natural or threatened loyalties to their functional managers pulling silo strings. The functional contributors danced to the matriced requirements only when the top management pulled the strings as the management layer above the functional level only is responsible for the enterprise objectives. This layer is normally the general management or the board in most enterprises. They take the decisions related to the enterprise objectives and are collectively responsible for the strategic and long-term results. Others below their stratospheric levels were forced to believe that they had no right to think of the strategic as they are normally asked to focus on their specialism roles. In such an environment, only the top management could become leader managers while scores or hundreds of managers in an organization got relegated to live the life of mere executioners, naturally driven by short-term goals and desire for lower needs gratification.

The overworked top management spews out the 'top down or decided upon' objectives and expects the results to be delivered by the functional and matrix structures like an intricate electronic circuit. Electronic products are normally driven by standard software. They call it the firmware, which dies with the product as it is meant for predetermined standard applications. Such standard structures and expectations can work in stable processes and environment. Changing contexts would need at least the firmware to be changed if not the hardware too. But, this firmware resides in the minds of the functional managers who are only or mostly responsible for their silo or specialism KPIs. Some managements draw consolation by adding enterprise KPIs expecting silo managers to be driven by the overall results, not realizing that hazy objectives can work only for the volitionally driven not those who have been relegated to their motivational prisons. When a tsunami strikes or malfunctioning mutterings surface in such organizations, the poor top management has to swoop in and douse fires or apply Band-Aid. Hence, functional matrix structures are anti-growth. They can be excellent for standard work processes running under modern day practice as per Taylor's management principles.

Then why do matrix structures prevail even after decades of decadent results? The only reason for this appears to be hesitation on part of the top management who shy away from delegating decision making powers for enterprise objectives or matriced results to lower levels and expect only execution of their decisions from others. Sadly, growth is about change management and this can only be managed by leader managers not faceless matrices or silo specialists. Change management is about leadership decisions that come from strategic objectives aligned to the vision and mission of the enterprise. In organizations, where the top management retains the right to take leadership decisions, Growth Management can only be their responsibility. Individuals with leadership genes from their foundation would either atrophy into unhappy automatons or just walk away.

2. Globalization and Socio-economic Disparity

Most companies before venturing out of their native markets have tasted success in their countries before they were forced to globalize due to falling demands, rising costs, competition, and opportunity for growth. The mother company and its subsidiary in another country may run the same business, but in largely different contexts.

The differences lie not only in cost per effort or language, but more importantly in the material quality of life, infrastructure, social security, and relationships. All these lead to a markedly different attitude to work and life in general. Managers from countries with such wide gaps owing to their socio-economic differences are prone to making judgments about the other side and end up in serious unspoken conflicts. That when combined with the functional or top management being from one country or region leaves the managers on the other side with not much scope for becoming leader managers. Most enterprises that hit the globalization stage face the above conflicts. They console themselves with running 'inter-cultural trainings' to bridge their self-perceived cultural gap instead of accepting the gaps arising out of socio-economic disparities or that from expectations not fulfilled due to non-alignment in purpose identification.

Economically developed countries of the west have a relatively flatter society and more independence in individual existence. Developing countries like India, where economic interdependence prevails, still live in the joint family system, albeit in reducing numbers. People in organizations come from different parts of the multi layered socio-economic strata and carry their social customs and habits into their work manifestations. Managers from the economically advanced countries with flatter societies and lesser dependence on family see these manifestations as hierarchical or feudal. Either they feign ignorance or they do not comprehend or come out as more egalitarian than the local managers. In India, a lot of younger colleagues still address me as 'Sir'. I am sure, I must have been perceived as a British lord by my western friends who encountered this for the first time. I did not always get the opportunity to explain to all my visitors that 'Sir' conveys respect for an elder in Indian society. In Indian languages, no elderly person is addressed without a respectful suffix to their name. On the other hand, expat managers returning to their home countries after a few years in India miss not only the Indian cuisine but also the social perks of Indian managerial life that they gladly enjoyed due to the cheap supply of labour for menial tasks.

Developing economies is where the rate of growth is the highest and participants in this growth are mostly knowledge workers and managers. Aspirational intents run much higher in developing societies due to the growth potential of the individual, both socio-economically and professionally. The yearning for a better quality of life makes people hungry for learning more as they know that is the best way to improve their quality of life. Yes, it is fertile ground for high voltage motivational engagement, hopefully more intrinsic in nature than extrinsic. Managers from developed societies do not have that high aspirational gaps to fulfil and may not be that much intrinsically motivated to learn anew unless it is to excel in their domain knowledge or skills. Managers on either side of the divide need to learn the power of empathy to understand the other and why the other side thinks, behaves, and acts in the way they do.

It is the same socio-economic gap that possibly makes managers from developing societies more likely to dream of remarkable achievements, be risk friendly, and ready to jump into their relative complexities—great potential for growth management. Managers from developed societies on the other hand are more inclined to be looking for perfection, effectiveness and efficiency. When such disparate mindsets have to work together, there is a natural divide and conflict. The managers from the developing societies need and therefore believe in faster progress and find their developed counterparts slow, deliberate, and bureaucratic. The mother company managers as the functional managers or seniors find their developing counterparts error prone, non trustworthy and withdraw more and more. On the other hand, managers in a developing society fail to empathize or to understand the delay in decision making and investments. As a result, the managers from developing societies get farther and farther from decision making, fail to find the rationale for decisions taken and bear the brunt of execution tasks only. The result is top down approach, lack of trust and an imposed culture of expectations to be fulfilled, ending up into a typical leader–manager divide that throttles growth management potential.

3. Cash is King, But Does Not Produce Growth

A management driven by motivational engagement cannot nurture the above leader managers. Most management loses its way due to an obsessive pursuit of the short-term economic performance of the enterprise instead of sustainable growth management. Sustainability comes from being able to create resources including financial resources. Any enterprise that produced cash but not enough leaders to deploy it for further growth, results in stagnation. Cash does not produce growth. It is leader managers who use the cash to create options and actions for sustainable growth. A management that creates cash may be considered darlings of the stock market only to be discarded as the dark horses when the bourses realize the lack of leadership to utilize the same for sustained profitable growth. Many successful companies wake up to the fact that they do not have enough managers who have the leadership mettle to create future growth. This happens to companies who have invested in developing good managerial skills to run efficiency, effectiveness, productivity but not in developing leadership. They realize the paradox only to struggle with the dilemma of importing leadership that is foreign to its culture. The risk is organizational hara-kiri or a purge of its committed resources.

The sea of complexity beckons the leader manager with managerial wisdom, not just skills. The forces of the LCD Syndrome and unbridled use of motivation theory with a masochistic dependency on pecuniary benefits has only added to the challenge by making wisdom increasingly an endangered species. Leader managers are available in abundance if only one has the eye for the foundation and provision for proper construction of their personalities. Let a potential leader manager get a whiff of complexity challenges in his or her domain and you can sit back and enjoy the miracles that ensue. All the leadership values of creativity, innovation, greatness, ethics, empathy, vision, mission, social responsibility, and growth management will follow. Romance will return to enterprises and the society will become a happier state to be in.

PART 6

In Reflection

Reflection is not usual for the young. For the old, it may become the only occupation. In the afternoon of my life as a manager, I find myself reflecting quite often. Is it good for me or not, time will tell. For the moment, I am happy to share my reflections on life in general for those I care for and respect. For you all, my readers.

- *The Trajectory of a Boss, a Manager, or a Leader*
- *That's My Way*

1
Trajectory of a Boss, a Manager, a Leader

> *'I believe that I am not responsible for the meaningfulness or meaninglessness of life, but that I am responsible for what I do with the life I've got.'*
>
> HERMANN HESSE

The Boss is a label I abhorred most of my life, probably because my father never 'bossed' me. When I became a boss to others (late 80s), my upbringing possibly made me not to go by the more prevalent 'command and control' management style of those days. Of course, I did not know such management jargon at that time.

I did not make any choices or pick up a management book to try different styles and see what gives me the best results. I just did what I did as per my habits from; my formative years. I carried the imprints as above all through the last three decades of my working life and discarded the label boss quite willingly while accepting the label manager or even leader with responsibility and humility.

I was also an elder brother and kind of inherited the legacy of my father as the head of the family. While I didn't have to 'command and control' in its today's pejorative nuance, I did have to take decisions at cross roads or in situations of conflict and my family followed me. I must have believed then that I did right for all in my family and its larger and long term interests. In hindsight, I realize that I did not do right all the time. I did make mistakes. Even in that phase of younger adulthood, I was conscious that my decisions did hurt some of my family members at different junctures.

First Phase

The above experience is akin to the 1st phase of my life as a manager or a leader. I had to take decisions and took on the responsibility to judge and decide the best for all concerned. The others followed; doing what I asked of them and not really questioning me or my decisions. At times they were a bit hesitant or unsure of their capabilities, but I could motivate them with my energy, confidence and by leading from the front. I could take care of their needs (quite basic relatively) and make up for their skill or knowledge deficits, if any, with some extra efforts on my part. This 1st phase was pretty busy and gratifying for me as I was the principal actor and major value creator. Few entitlements and prerogatives did not do much harm to my self esteem.

Second Phase

Soon I was confronted with situations where the apprenticeship under my father (org-speak: my experience) did not give me all the answers as the context changed gradually but surely. My father passed away too early for me to get all the 'case studies'. I had to invent or discover my own way. I had to envisage and decide on future perspectives and goals for the family and lead the way. In org-speak, one would call this an exercise in building the 'vision' and deciding on the 'mission'. The vision helped to look for and choose options, while the sense of the mission paved the way for what not to do or engage in. The culture of the family or the organization was bred and nurtured governed by the vision and mission.

The members of my family (team) were growing up fast and developed their own opinions too, at times a bit radical in my view. I explained why I took the decisions I did. The more they grew, the more I explained. I was still the boss—the explaining type, not the commanding type. In retrospect, I see that these explanations helped me refine my thinking and honed my rationale for the decisions I took. I was mostly intuitive in my decisions. The explanations acted as a 'rational filter' and at times made me change my tactics if not the objectives or decisions.

Third Phase

Thereafter came the time when I shifted from auto to manual mode of decision making. I started engaging the adult (grown up) members before I took decisions. It was fun, throwing ideas at them, getting contradicted when not agreeable, listening to their arguments that I had not thought of, as I had not thought of the contradictions they came up with. I learnt a lot for the first time from my family (team) members. My mind enlarged and even sharpened as I had to debate with sharp enough minds but yet take decisions. At the end they respected my decisions even if not agreeing at times as we had a tremendous bonding based on trust and mutual respect.

But, these debates and subsequent decision making/actions (manual mode) needed much more time than the auto (intuitive decisions followed by action and explanations) mode of the 2nd phase. It needed some real hard work from all of us, but it was still enjoyable and positive in most respects.

However, the process of decision making had become more arduous and leading from the front became more of a liability than an asset for the family (team). I became the bottleneck, the biggest cause of inefficiency. The potential was more than what I could crunch alone. I needed more leaders than doers. I needed to do things differently now although I was still the boss. I started taking risks I had not taken earlier. I allowed/ encouraged some of the grown-ups (best team members) to take their decisions and act on their own. It was not easy for them.

The trick I learnt to play with consistency was to just make myself unavailable for them to find their way of deciding and doing things on their own. The family grew, the organization developed, and few more leaders emerged to lead from the front.

Fourth Phase

The family (organization) became a bit large and complex. Self-actualization needs of each individual became more and more pronounced. Independence in fulfilling responsibilities came around with strengths developed by members to handle the same. Differences in perspectives and choices widened. Obviously, decisions had to be taken by them and not by me anymore. But, somehow I still remained the head of the family. It is a funny experience, more like the head of a federation than a unit entity. I had no experience for this and had not any imprints to draw inspiration from. But I knew I had to withdraw, resist my impulse to decide, or act on responsibilities taken over by others.

The problem was that they were not others, they were my team, my family members; yes, they were now like me—grown up adults, capable and bursting with energy and yearning to work things out their way. Their ways could be at times different to how I would have done it, but I had faith in the concept that they had to find their way and succeed. I had to let go and find some other things to do.

Like most Indians, I had also grown up listening to the epic stories that form the basis for what could be called as Indian philosophy. I was aware of the four stages of life as prescribed by the Vedic scriptures—*Bhramacharya* (learning stage), *Grihashtha* (building and consumption stage), *Vanaprastha* (when you let go and make yourself available for guidance), and *Sanyasa* (when you retire from active life and prepare for death). I was intellectually prepared for *vanaprastha*, but not emotionally or physically. I decided to put my theoretical awareness into practice and learn while in practice. It was exhilarating to begin with and sometimes frustrating or boring as time went by. The habits of old were not of much help. New habits of thinking needed to be developed. It was during this phase that philosophy became a more important teacher for me than science.

I had to find a definition for my new head of the family role. I struggled for some time, but found it in due course. Transition and transition management became my responsibility, instead of execution. In *vanaprastha*, one needs to take decisions too but only for what one has to do with the responsibility of transition management in mind. In the world we live in today, we live longer or have to live longer due to several factors. The challenge lies in filling up the space between *vanaprastha* and *sanyasa* or between the 4th phase and the point 'B' in the graphic below. But, while the decline to 'B'—*sanyasa*—as the last phase of life (sigmoid curve) as per Vedic teachings is quite logical, the speed at which *vanaprastha* hits some of us or the sheer length of life that we need to live, asks for a 5th phase before the curtains can finally come down.

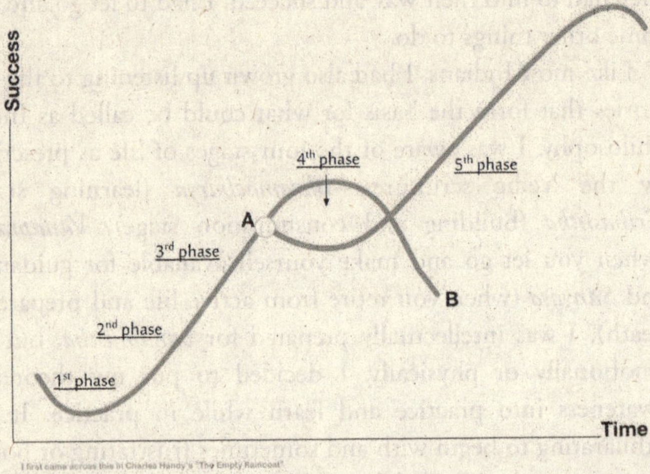

FIG. 18 – THE SIGMOID CURVE AND THE 5TH PHASE

Fifth Phase

Like in Kotler's product life cycle, the 5th phase has become a necessity for a lot of fortunate ones like me, if only to straddle the longevity of life or because *vanaprastha* hits us much earlier than we can afford to slide into oblivion towards the point B. While my *vanaprastha* had to go on in reducing volumes, I was in desperate need of a product feature or a new market that could give me my fifth phase. The hunt was on.

Lucky as I have been most of my life, an additional responsibility came my way. It was something totally foreign to my habits. Therefore, it was interesting enough as I got another chance to learn something new. In this additional role, neither was I the head of a federated family nor was I on the *vanaprasthic* pulpit. I have to get things done together with others who are also responsible for the same objectives. The interesting thing is that the objectives too are not crystal clear. We have to learn, create, and execute the objectives simultaneously. It is a new search; it is a new thirst. The habits developed so far makes me mostly behave as a pendulum between my 3rd phase role and the 4th phase. I know very well that habits die hard and I have to find my answers that fit my fifth phase.

2
That's My Way

Why not live again? Why not laugh again? why not have fun again? Why not live the same organizational life that I was blessed to lead for the last 30 years? Well, almost 90 percent of those years was fun, was a challenge, and was a life worth living, full of unknown bends, knowing not what lay ahead, carpet bagging all the way.

I know that the term carpetbagger has a pejorative bent to it. So what? When I hit the road as a 'sales guy' over 30 years back, that label too was no less pejorative. It was respectable to be an engineer, a doctor, or a government officer. A sales guy was someone who could not match up to these professions. For me, I did not even try to be one since the flooding waters of life swept me to the dusty and grimy lanes of selling and I had no choice but to survive. And yes, like many, I did and I did it my way.

Every time I looked in temerity around the corner, spread out in front was an uncharted jungle that I knew not. I gingerly took my first steps forward with my carpet bag of philosophy and the need for moving ahead. With every sortie, I learnt more than I knew before. But, each time I ended up getting bored with what I did well in. I sniffed around for more that could challenge me with its limits. I was always lucky to find some barriers, some challengers, mostly worth their name in salt. I moved from one trade to another, from one industry to the other, and later from one function to another or from one domain of boredom (some may call it comfort) to another land of unknowns only to be rewarded with new hurdles, new enlightenment, and always ended up with a more developed identity.

Most importantly, it was a journey that always left me enriched with greater understanding, empathy, knowledge, and experiences of discovering new opportunities. I met so many people, so many interesting, intelligent and vibrant personalities, who became my friends, my associates, my inspiration, my leaders, my protégées, and teachers. My parents and my society had given me the culture to respect greatness, knowledge, and capability. I have been so lucky all these years to find so many whom I could respect, spar with, learn from, and measure up to.

Last few years, I took a breather, allowed by my organization—I thank their wisdom—till it became quite a weight on my bored shoulders. My mind repeatedly raced into thoughts to unshackle myself from this 'breather'. All around me were younger people, a lot of them who had grown up with me. I enjoyed the shade while they were romping on between horizons. I tried to regale myself with their successes, their trysts with their destinies, offering them scholarly advice when they stopped by. My children too were growing up and it was likewise a joy to usher them on and pester them with my foresights borne out of my hindsight.

I almost started enjoying my *vanaprastha*—the third of the four stages of human life prescribed by Vedantic scriptures—only to be shaken once in a while by the thought that I was not yet ready to wrap up, I had still years to live, but not with many ideas how to do that. At this juncture, a realization started crystallizing in my mind—I was not really so much required by most in my advisory role; like my grown up children, some had moved on and many were almost at the threshold of breaking free.

I wrestled with this artificial *vanaprastha*. I huffed and puffed, I lectured and pontificated, I held court and berated. I gradually sensed the impatience of my erstwhile followers and peers. I concluded that I need to break free as *vanaprastha* did not belong in an organization. An organization is about *grihastha*—the second stage of human life, where one's Karma is to build, create, and consume. I decided to return to *brahmacharya*—the first stage of human life, that of a student—and register for a PhD I knew was not going to be easy. I knew it would be a path full of hurdles and hardship, particularly for my age and stage of life when I still had some more responsibilities to fulfil. But, the mere thought of such obstacles fired up the embers in my mind. I was alive again—ready to haul up my carpet bag. Started dusting the bag up and was just getting ready, when like of the old, came an offer to start another innings in organizational existence. I was flummoxed for a while! I had given up organizational life in my mind for some time and to live it again was like going back to *grihastha*.

My appointment with the professor I wanted to do a PhD with was still a month away and hence was not really an option. The new role offered in my organization was about something I relished in the years gone by—to create, to build, to develop—to live for a dream. So what if I was not in the circuit for some time? So what if I did not know all that had transpired in the meanwhile. So what if I was not clear about what exactly needs to be done. That is what I had always done all these years—peeking around the bends, jumping into uncertainties, playing with risks, and making something out of unknowns. That was my way.

Somewhere deep in my mind I had a sense of guilt. Should I be excited again when so many youngsters are there waiting for their chance to take the bull by its horns? Do I deserve to be happy again in the same way as earlier while so many have their aspirations in the budding phase? For the first time in my life, I slept over the decision to jump out of the corner into the new lanes of life. For the first time in my life, I conferred with my family and friends.

I finally succumbed. Made my creaky self stand up again. The engine sputtered and muttered, but stayed on. The steering shivered for a few days, but now drives steady. The gears were rusty, but caught on. But, one thing IS different. I know this would be the last flutter, the last organizational corner I jump out from. *Grihastha* if it has to be, so it will be...for a few more years.

I thank all those who taught me without my knowing, the art of jumping out from the corner, hitting the new lanes on the run, and finding a home of serendipity. Habits die hard and I am no exception.

It is back to old ways – living Beyond Expectations!

Why Beyond Expectations! [31]

Expectations of your family, friends, employers, employees, customers, competitors, and of your own are all Limitations. Living

[31] My first workshop under the banner 'Beyond Expectations' happened in March 2002, when my friend, the MD of Lufthansa Cargo Charter GmbH, invited me to do a facilitation for his management team—his ask was to make them think beyond their habits of old.

within these limitations could be normal and satisfactory for many but there are some people who are leaders as per this author who have preferred to lead their lives 'beyond expectations'. Most people before being corrupted or reduced to the Lowest Common Denominator (LCD) by the constraints of their perceived reality have ambitions, aspirations, dreams and even the will to achieve their goals. Even before fatalism sets in for some, the rigours of the short-term make most people settle for compromises or 'satisfactory underperformance'. Habits formed through living under such limitations are then manifested in how an individual approaches or views the challenges or opportunities thrown up by life at large.

The majority is either oblivious of such individuals living beyond expectations or marvel at them while a minority try to play the catch up game without getting out of their habit forming experiential funnels. Psychologists have proven time and again that the environment in which an individual is imprisoned is largely responsible for its behaviour and cognizance levels. Yet, most organizations, managers and leaders exhort others to 'change' without changing the environment or even their own manifestations. Yes, it is either hypocrisy or the short-term comfort of such entities that make them resort to such apparent stupidity.

Acknowledgements

I have been lucky in four things to start with—the day I was born, the parents I was born to, the place I was born in, and the kind of human being I was reared as. Hence, I dedicate this book to my parents—Pradyot Narayan Chatterjee and Suniti Chatterjee—who gave me the foundation on which I stand today and will, forever.

Since this is a management practitioner's book, the insights I gained in management of people and organization is an accumulation of all that I subconsciously and consciously absorbed working with hundreds of different and most interesting people all my years. I was particularly fortunate in being influenced by my one–time followers like Amit Sharma, Mohan Bhat, Govindraju, Bharathi BK, Krishna Rao, Anthony Joseph Prakash, Prakash Karunakaran, Bhimasen Vadavi, Sujith Naranthatta, and Prabhakar Sivaramakrishnan to name a few. All the above colleagues had no choice but to listen to everything I wrote and give me their feedback. If it was not for Amit Sharma, this book may have remained just a still born idea. He always egged me on to write and share my story on management learning. Thank you Amit and Mohan for always being there to listen to my thoughts and articles and challenging me in everything I did.

You neither choose your parents nor your managers and one always learns a lot from their manager's leadership behaviour. Two of my managers who influenced me the most with their entirely different personalities and styles are Cherian Philip and Volker Niebel. Cherian Philip taught me in one sentence the significance of being a manager and gave me the opportunity to learn and develop my way. My belief in the value of trust, faith, respect, and interdependence in management was best corroborated in the years of working with my current manager, Volker Niebel, the Executive Vice President and Member of GEC, Sartorius Group, Germany. I am also grateful to the Board of Sartorius AG that gave me the opportunity to express my choices and contribute in my way to the organization. Dr Joachim Kreuzburg, CEO of the Sartorius Group and Reinhard Vogt, Member of the Board of Sartorius AG have been exemplary influences on me with their consistency and vision of the long term. My partner in building up Sartorius India over the last eight years, Dr Oscar-Werner Reif, Executive Vice President and Member of the GEC, has been one of the most dedicated individuals I have worked with in my entire life. It has always been a pleasure and learning while matching wits in details and speed with Oscar.

Working with my peers and academics has been my good fortune for the last 13 years. I would like to particularly name Profs. S. Venkatesh of AIT, Bangkok and Ramnath Narayanswamy of the IIM, Bangalore, Prof. Quy Ngyuen Huy of INSEAD and my international colleagues like Peter Grimley, Dr Bodo Krebs, Kirsten Siedler, Dr Thorsten Peuker, Matthias Wessel, Reinhard Baumfalk, and Uwe Becker. Each of them at times has been a teacher, a case study, and a sharp mind that helped me hone my observations, apply them, and correct them. I express my deepest gratitude to my very special friends and senior managers from the industry—Liliane De Lassus, Daney Wilkinson, Kirsten Siedler, Dr Joerg Lindenblatt, Oliver Hahn, and Mark Hirst who took time off from their normal busy routines to read the manuscript and offer me their most valuable critiques.

I wish to specially thank Prof. Jonathan Gosling, Director of Leadership, Exeter University, and Co-founder of the IMPM for agreeing to write the foreword for this book. Jonathan will always remain a beacon of encouragement and wisdom for me. I'd like to thank Radhika Marwah, my editor at Random House. My idea of an editor was completely turned on its head by this extremely intelligent, smiling but sharp young lady. Radhika's questions and prompts made the book more lucid. She probably wanted more but at the end we had to call a truce.

I had to leave it for the end to acknowledge the love, faith, and perseverance of my dear wife Arpita who also taught me very important tenets of management; after all she has been managing me for the last 26 years. Our children, Kirit and Antara, have been the joy and challenge for us and we are lucky to have them as strong individuals on whom we have been consistently experimenting our parenting art without them complaining much. Even they had to learn all what I learnt while they had to do their homework on their own and go through colleges. Today, while they are embarking on their journey of life, I just hope with eyes shut that I could learn enough from my life to have given them a good enough foundation to blossom into happiness and treasure it.

A Note on the Author

Amit is the Managing Director of the Sartorius India group of companies since 2002. He has been with the company since 1993. Sartorius AG (www.sartorius.com), is a 140-year-old German technology major listed on the German and French stock exchanges. A post graduate in Chemistry, Amit has a diploma in Practising Management (*IMPM; www.impm.org*) from INSEAD, France and a Master of Management from McGill University, Canada. His professional repertoire includes 15 years in Sales and Marketing and 17 years in Strategic Management.

Amit is a certified Leadership Trainer for international managers for the Sartorius Group worldwide. His passion lies in people development, organization design, growth management, and inter-cultural cooperation between Indo-European groups. Amit has been a guest faculty at AIT Business School, Bangkok and at the Indian Institute of Management, Bangalore, where he taught a 3-Credit course on *Leadership & Change Management.* He does workshops on invitation on associated topics for senior management and leadership of various organizations. He devotes at least four days a month as a Growth Facilitator under the banner, *Beyond Expectations* mentoring young graduates, managers and organizations as an activity to top up his volitional energy (*www.beyondex.in*).

Amit loves to build new organizations and derives great satisfaction from instigating growth in individuals. He loves to interact with people from different backgrounds, beliefs and experiences as this adds to his knowledge and experience. Although, he has an academic background in science, he believes in philosophy, psychology and economics being the most important tenets to invest in, to become a successful human being. He relaxes most among books and makes it his business to discuss what he learns with his family, friends and associates.

Amit lives in Bangalore with his mother, wife and two children and strives to give back to the society what little he can in order to make his life more meaningful.

